TABLE OF CON

MW00889648

MOUNT RUSHMORE

Mountain of Presidents

If you travel through the western part of South Dakota, you might see four huge heads looking at you. These heads are made of rock, but they were not made by nature. They form a monument called Mount Rushmore.

A sculptor named Gutzon Borglum built Mount Rushmore. He chose four presidents he thought were symbols of America: George Washington, Thomas Jefferson, Abraham Lincoln, and Theodore Roosevelt.

Borglum's workers started creating the monument in 1927. Workers drilled holes in the granite rock and placed dynamite in them to blow the rock apart. They dynamited 450,000 tons of rock from the mountain. Then stonecutters moved in to carve the stone into faces. Dynamiting was so dangerous that all the workers had to leave the mountain during blasting. This safety precaution was worth it. No one was killed during construction.

Borglum drew plans of what the monument would look like. However, the mountain did not always cooperate. Sometimes the rock was cracked or too soft to use. When this happened, Borglum had to change his plans. He changed them nine times!

Mount Rushmore was a tourist attraction even before it was finished. Thousands of people came to watch it being built. Finally, the monument was completed in the fall of 1941. Today, more than two million people visit the site every year to see the amazing sight of four presidents looking out of a mountain.

Show What You Know!

Write whether each statement is *true* or *false*.

1 _____ Mount Rushmore is a natural formation.

2 _____ Workers dynamited 450,000 tons of rock from the mountain.

3 _____ Many workers were killed during construction.

4 _____ It took fewer than 10 years to complete Mount Rushmore.

5 _____ Mount Rushmore is a popular tourist attraction.

6 _____ Mount Rushmore is more than 60 years old.

7 _____ Borglum's plans never had to be changed.

8 _____ The presidents on Mount Rushmore are symbols of America.

Use the information in the story to name the presidential faces on Mt. Rushmore.

HINT: Theodore Roosevelt had a mustache.

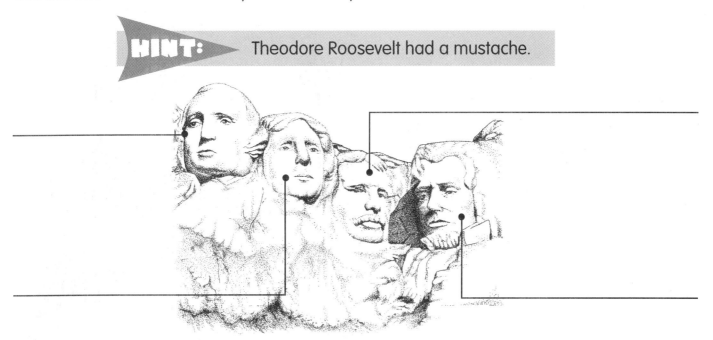

WORD SQUARES

Each square below contains an eight-letter word from the story. Find each word by starting at one of the letters and reading either clockwise or counterclockwise.

T A I
N   N
U O M

_____

O E H
D   T
O R E

_____

E R U
R   S
O M H

_____

M I T
A   E
N Y D

_____

C U L
S   P
R O T

_____

M T N
O   E
N U M

_____

CHALLENGE

Find more eight-letter words and make your own word squares.

U.S. Facts & Fun • EMC 6306 • ©2005 by Evan-Moor Corp.

The A-Maze-ing MOUNTAIN

These tourists want to explore Mount Rushmore. Can you help them find their way through the mountain maze?

DAVY CROCKETT
King of the Wild Frontier

I KILLED 105 BEARS IN 7 MONTHS!

YEAH... RIGHT!!

Davy Crockett was called the "King of the Wild Frontier." This amazing man was born in eastern Tennessee in 1786. His father ran a tavern, and Davy loved to hear the stories of travelers who stopped there. Someday, he told himself, he would explore the wilderness and have his own adventures.

When Crockett was a teenager, he got into a fight at school. He knew his father would be angry with him for fighting. So instead of going home, he got a job driving a herd of cattle to Virginia. Crockett had to protect himself and his cattle. He learned many skills that helped him survive in the wilderness before he returned home two years later.

Crockett did not have much education or money. He knew a lot of Americans were just like him, and he wanted to help them. In 1820, Crockett was elected to the Tennessee legislature. Later, he became a U.S. Congressman. He helped pass laws so settlers could keep their land. Crockett often told people, "Be always sure you're right; then go ahead."

During the 1830s, Texas was fighting for independence from Mexico. Crockett volunteered for the Texas army and was sent to a fort called the Alamo. On March 6, 1836, the Mexican army attacked the fort and killed everyone inside.

Davy Crockett's death shocked the nation. Songs were written about him. Later, movies were made about his life. This American hero lives on today in the nation's adventurous spirit.

U.S. Facts & Fun • EMC 6306 • ©2005 by Evan-Moor Corp.

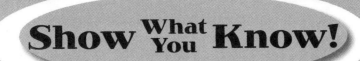

Number these events in the order in which they happened.

_____ Crockett became a U.S. Congressman.

_____ Crockett got a job driving cattle.

_____ Crockett ran away from home after a fight.

_____ Crockett was killed defending the Alamo.

_____ Movies were made about Crockett's life.

_____ Crockett was elected to the Tennessee legislature.

_____ Crockett listened to stories at his father's tavern.

_____ Crockett volunteered for the Texas army.

CHALLENGE

Write another detail about Davy Crockett's life. What two numbers would it come between in the above sequence?

_____

_____

_____

_____

It would come between number _____ and number _____ .

HIDDEN PICTURES

When he lived in the wilderness, Davy Crockett had to hunt to survive.
Can you find six hidden animals in the forest below? Color them.

U.S. Facts & Fun • EMC 6306 • ©2005 by Evan-Moor Corp.

DAVY CROCKETT SCRAMBLE

Unscramble the words below and write them on the lines. Then unscramble the shaded letters to find out what item of clothing Crockett was famous for wearing.

HINT: The number after each scrambled word tells you the paragraph where the word can be found.

NESESETNE (1) ___ ___ ___ ___ ___ ___ ___ ___ ___

LTACTE (2) ___ ___ ___ ___ ___ ___

ECNEEDNPENID (4)

___ ___ ___ ___ ___ ___ ___ ___ ___ ___ ___ ___

REOFITNR (1) ___ ___ ___ ___ ___ ___ ___ ___

KLSSLI (2) ___ ___ ___ ___ ___ ___

LOAMA (4) ___ ___ ___ ___ ___

XCEMOI (4) ___ ___ ___ ___ ___ ___

Shaded letters: ___ ___ ___ ___ ___ ___ ___ ___ ___ ___ ___ ___ ___

Item of Clothing: ___ ___ ___ n s ___ ___ ___ ___ p

Adding STARS to the FLAG

Each star on the American flag stands for one of the 50 states. Every time a state is added, the flag's design is changed.

In 1958, a high-school student named Robert Heft was doing a history project. At that time, there were 48 states. Alaska and Hawaii would soon be added. That meant that the American flag would need two more stars. Heft decided to design a new flag.

Heft took the family flag and cut out the stars. He made two more stars out of white iron-on tape. Then he arranged all the stars. He alternated rows of six stars with rows of five stars.

When Heft brought his flag to school, his teacher gave him a poor grade because the flag had too many stars. When Heft complained, his teacher told him to get the U.S. Congress to approve his design if he wanted a better grade.

Heft was angry. He went to see his Congressman and explained what had happened. The congressman agreed to present the design to Congress.

In 1960, a new flag featuring Robert Heft's design flew for the first time over the U.S. Capitol in Washington, D.C. Heft stood next to President Dwight D. Eisenhower at the ceremony.

Heft's teacher kept the promise he had made two years earlier. He finally gave Robert Heft the "A" he deserved.

The 13 red and white stripes stand for the 13 original states. The blue field has a star for each of the 50 states. Rows of six stars alternate with rows of five stars.

Show What You Know!

Complete the crossword puzzle using words from the story.

Across

1. Robert Heft designed a new flag for his ___ ___ ___ ___ ___ ___ ___ class.

5. Today's flag has ___ ___ ___ ___ ___ stars.

6. In 1958, the American flag had

   ___ ___ ___ ___ ___ — ___ ___ ___ ___ ___ stars.

7. The last two states admitted to the U.S. were ___ ___ ___ ___ ___ ___ and Hawaii.

Down

2. Robert Heft's ___ ___ ___ ___ ___ ___ ___ gave him a poor grade at first.

3. The ___ ___ ___ ___ ___ on the flag represent the states.

4. Heft's design was approved by the U.S. ___ ___ ___ ___ ___ ___ ___ .

STARRY CODE

Use the numbered code below to figure out the name of a famous song about the U.S. flag.

12 x 12 = ____ = A

78 + 54 = ____ = D

51 − 36 = ____ = E

19 x 3 = ____ = F

62 + 89 = ____ = H

13 x 13 = ____ = I

92 − 27 = ____ = N

109 − 64 = ____ = O

25 + 216 = ____ = P

269 + 47 = ____ = R

16 x 14 = ____ = S

219 − 138 = ____ = T

54 x 3 = ____ = V

____ ____ ____   ____ ____ ____ ____ ____   ____ ____ ____
81   151   15   224   81   144   316   224   144   65   132

____ ____ ____ ____ ____ ____ ____   ____ ____ ____ ____ ____ ____ ____
224   81   316   169   241   15   224   57   45   316   15   162   15   316

U.S. Facts & Fun • EMC 6306 • ©2005 by Evan-Moor Corp.

The First U.S. FLAG

On June 14, 1777, Congress announced that the United States flag would have 13 red and white stripes and 13 white stars on a blue background. Today, we celebrate June 14 as Flag Day. Congress did not say how the stars should be arranged, so different flags used different designs. As new states joined the nation, each one demanded its own star.

Can you find each of the original 13 states in the word search? The name of each state is listed below. After you find each state, color the star next to its name. Be sure to look in all directions!

```
A Z R E E L H K H N R E A A P
F N Z H Q R R A E D R S I N C
D P I K O O A W C I V L N I O
P X P L Y D J W H W H X I L N
L A D W O E E S A U P B G O N
A P E U R R P I B L V Y R R E
P N L S L M A C S K E K I A C
N C E Z A H L C V L K D V C T
G Y Z H E Z C B H G A B E H I
B A W O L D F F H T U N F T C
L E D N A L Y R A M R T D U U
N G E O R G I A W Q M O Y O T
Q R N V G A E C H Z J K N S R
S T T E S U H C A S S A M U I
P E N N S Y L V A N I A V X C
```

☆ CONNECTICUT   ☆ DELAWARE   ☆ GEORGIA   ☆ VIRGINIA

☆ MARYLAND   ☆ MASSACHUSETTS   ☆ NEW HAMPSHIRE

☆ NEW JERSEY   ☆ NEW YORK   ☆ NORTH CAROLINA

☆ PENNSYLVANIA   ☆ RHODE ISLAND   ☆ SOUTH CAROLINA

Declaring Independence

On July 4, 1776, church bells rang in the city of Philadelphia. The Declaration of Independence had been accepted by the Continental Congress. The United States said it was no longer ruled by Great Britain.

Thomas Jefferson had less than three weeks to write the Declaration of Independence. When he gave the document to the Continental Congress, Jefferson was asked to make some changes. He had to change 47 words or phrases and add 3 new paragraphs. Congress then made 39 more changes to the document! Jefferson wasn't happy about these changes, but he did what the men asked.

The Declaration said that "all men are created equal" and everyone had the right to "life, liberty, and the pursuit of happiness." No one could take these rights away, not even a king. The Declaration listed all the unfair things the British king had done. Finally, it said the colonies were a free nation.

It took more than words for Americans to win their freedom. The Americans fought the British until 1783. Then a peace treaty was signed in Paris to end the war. Seven years after Thomas Jefferson declared the country's independence, the United States was truly free.

Answer each question.

1 How much time did Jefferson have to write the Declaration?

_____

2 How many changes and additions did Congress ask Jefferson to make?

_____

3 How did Jefferson feel when Congress changed what he had written? Why do you think he felt this way?

_____

_____

_____

4 What rights does the Declaration say everyone has?

_____

_____

5 When did the United States finally win its fight for freedom?

_____

Independence Kriss-Kross

Fit the following words from the story into the grid below.
We've put in the first word to get you started.

4-Letter Words
KING
LIFE

5-Letter Words
PEACE
WORDS

6-Letter Words
TREATY
UNFAIR

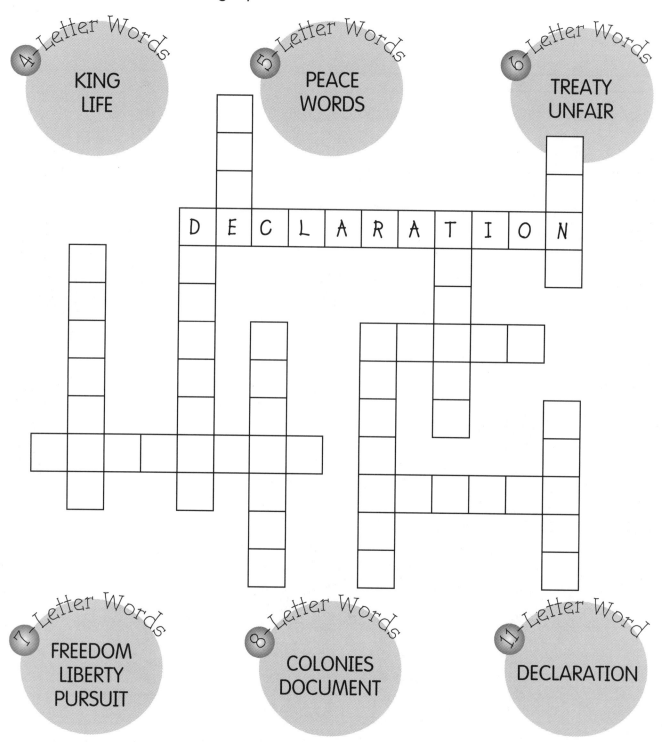

7-Letter Words
FREEDOM
LIBERTY
PURSUIT

8-Letter Words
COLONIES
DOCUMENT

11-Letter Word
DECLARATION

Hidden Quills

Thomas Jefferson wrote the Declaration of Independence with a quill pen. A quill pen is made from a bird's feather, or quill. The tip is dipped into ink in order to write.

Find and color seven quill pens hidden in the picture below.

George Washington Carver
MR. PEANUT

For 200 years, the most important crop grown in the southern United States was cotton. By the late 1800s, however, the soil was worn out from growing cotton every year. The farmers needed help. A black American scientist named George Washington Carver had the answer—peanuts!

Carver was a teacher who knew a lot about plants and farming. He worked at a school in Alabama called the Tuskegee Institute. Carver told the farmers to plant different crops besides cotton. Changing crops would make the soil healthy again. Carver suggested that the farmers plant peanuts.

Peanuts grew very well in Alabama. But the farmers didn't know what to do with their peanut crop. In those days, peanuts were only used as animal feed. No one thought they were good enough for people to eat.

Carver knew that lots of tasty things could be made from peanuts. One night, he invited his friends over for a special dinner. Every food, including soup, bread, and ice cream, was made from peanuts! Within a few years, peanuts were an important crop. During his lifetime, Carver found more than 300 ways to use peanuts. He truly was the original "Mr. Peanut."

Fill in the blanks with words from the story to complete each sentence below. Then put the numbered letters in order to spell the name of another food George Washington Carver found many uses for.

1 Cotton was the most popular crop in the ___ ___ ___ ___ ___ ___ ___
    United States.   **1**   **7**   **5**

2 Carver was a ___ ___ ___ ___ ___ ___ ___ at Tuskegee Institute.
     8   **3**

3 The Tuskegee Institute was in ___ ___ ___ ___ ___ ___ ___ .
           9

4 Originally, peanuts were only used to ___ ___ ___ ___ animals.
         4

5 Carver found more than 300 ___ ___ ___ ___ to use peanuts.
     2

6 Carver once made a whole meal out of ___ ___ ___ ___ ___ ___ ___ .
        6   **10**

7 Peanuts soon became an important ___ ___ ___ ___ .
        11

___ ___ ___ ___ ___   ___ ___ ___ ___ ___ ___
1   **2**   **3**   **4**   **5**   **6**   **7**   **8**   **9**   **10**   **11**

Spelling BEE

Use letters from George Washington Carver's name to spell the answers to the questions below. Each letter will be used only once, and all letters will be used.

HINT: Cross out each letter as you use it.

GEORGE WASHINGTON CARVER

1. Something to put flowers in   ___ ___ ___ ___

2. Opposite of *day*   ___ ___ ___ ___ ___

3. A large black bird   ___ ___ ___ ___

4. Something a hen lays   ___ ___ ___

5. Opposite of *far*   ___ ___ ___ ___

6. Abbreviation of *Oregon*   ___ ___

MORE Spelling FUN!

How many words with four or more letters can you make using the letters in the answer on page 19?

_____   _____

_____   _____

_____   _____

PEANUT MATCH-UP

Can you find the two jars of peanut butter that are the same? Circle them.

The Boston Tea Party— A **Wild** Affair

A tea party sounds like a quiet, elegant event. But one tea party that took place more than 230 years ago was not quiet and elegant at all! Instead, the event brought about the American Revolution.

People in the American colonies were angry when Great Britain placed a tax on tea. When ships loaded with tea arrived in Boston, Massachusetts, in November 1773, the American workers refused to unload them. The British said the Americans had to unload the tea and pay the tax by December 16.

That night, a huge crowd gathered in the city. Someone yelled, "Tonight Boston Harbor is a teapot!" A group of men disguised themselves as Native Americans. They led the crowd to the harbor.

The disguised colonists sneaked onto the three British ships. They dragged 342 chests of tea onto the decks. Then they broke the chests open and threw all the tea into the harbor.

The colonists had shown the British that they were not afraid to take action against unfair laws and taxes. Less than two years later, these actions would lead to war and—finally—independence.

Show What You Know!

Write whether each statement is true *(T)* or false *(F)*.

1 _____ The Boston Tea Party was a friendly meeting between the Americans and the British.

2 _____ British ships loaded with tea were docked in Boston Harbor.

3 _____ The colonists didn't mind paying taxes on tea.

4 _____ Some colonists disguised themselves as Native Americans before they went to the harbor.

5 _____ The colonists threw 342 chests of tea into the harbor.

6 _____ The Boston Tea Party was not an important event in American history.

7 _____ Less than two years after the Boston Tea Party, the colonies went to war against Great Britain.

8 _____ The colonists boarded two British ships.

Tea Party Maze

Help this colonist find his way back to shore. Find the correct path through the maze.

A Patriotic Dot-to-Dot

Connect the dots to see a portrait of an American patriot who lived in Boston at the time of the Boston Tea Party. This man later became the second president of the United States. Unscramble the letters to find his name.

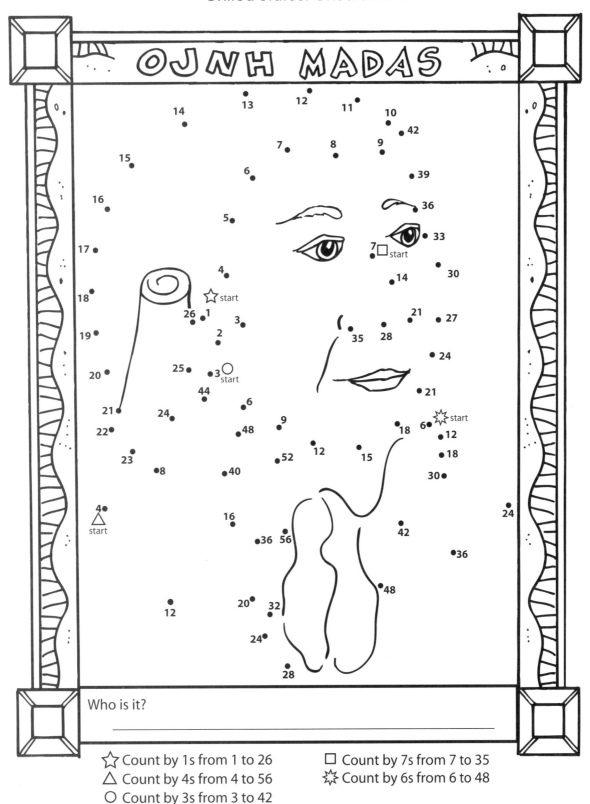

OJNH MADAS

Who is it?

_____

☆ Count by 1s from 1 to 26
△ Count by 4s from 4 to 56
○ Count by 3s from 3 to 42

☐ Count by 7s from 7 to 35
✹ Count by 6s from 6 to 48

Laura Ingalls Wilder
PIONEER GIRL

Laura Ingalls Wilder lived a life of adventure. She was born in a log cabin in Wisconsin in 1867. A few years later, the family moved to what is now Oklahoma. In those days, the area was known as Indian Territory. Indian Territory could be a very dangerous place. When Laura's father learned the U.S. government wouldn't protect people living there, he moved his family to De Smet, South Dakota. For a while, they lived in a sod house dug under the ground!

Laura was a smart girl, but she never graduated from high school. However, she was able to get a job as a teacher. When she was only 18, she quit her job to marry Almanzo Wilder.

Laura and Almanzo moved to a farm in Missouri. Laura cared for their daughter, Rose. She also wrote articles about farm life for the local newspaper.

When she was 65 years old, Laura published a book about her childhood. It was called *Little House in the Big Woods*. The book was so successful that Laura wrote many more books about life in the pioneer days. She kept writing until she died in 1957. She was 90 years old.

Laura's childhood was very different from the lives of children today. But millions of children have shared her world through her exciting stories.

U.S. Facts & Fun • EMC 6306 • ©2005 by Evan-Moor Corp.

Match each word from the story to its definition.

· ·

adventure	a large area of land
Indian	soil and grass
dangerous	to take care of
government	a Native American
sod	a small house
territory	writing published in a newspaper
protect	someone who lives in a new area
cabin	not safe
articles	an exciting or scary experience
pioneer	a group of people who rule a country

· ·

DRAWING FUN

Thousands of settlers journeyed west in covered wagons. Below, there is a picture of a covered wagon. Copy each square into the grid on page 29 to draw your own covered wagon! Then color the picture any way you'd like.

Copy each square from the picture on page 28 into the grid below to draw your own covered wagon! Then color the picture any way you'd like.

1	2	3	4	5	6	7
8	9	10	11	12	13	14
15	16	17	18	19	20	21
22	23	24	25	26	27	28
29	30	31	32	33	34	35
36	37	38	39	40	41	42
43	44	45	46	47	48	49

Totem Poles — Faces of Wood

Have you ever seen a totem pole? These tall wooden structures are very common in the northwestern part of the United States and Canada. Native Americans carved totem poles. The animals and other figures on the poles told stories about a family's history or stories from its culture.

Cedar is the best kind of wood to use for a totem pole. First, the tree is cut down. The bark is then cut off, and the tree is hollowed and shaped. Finally, the features are carved into the pole. Some poles are painted with bright colors.

Early Native Americans used sharpened shells, stones, or bones to carve their poles. Later, they used iron knives and other tools. Today, some carvers even use chain saws!

In the past, some totem poles were placed on the beach to welcome visitors to a village. Others were placed in front of the house. Sometimes, a totem pole was part of the house itself!

Native American society has changed a lot in the past 200 years. The art of carving totem poles was almost lost. Fortunately, museums and Native American societies have tried to keep the art of totem poles alive. Today, young carvers can still learn the art of creating a story out of wood.

U.S. Facts & Fun • EMC 6306 • ©2005 by Evan-Moor Corp.

Answer each question.

1 Where are totem poles commonly found?

_____

_____

2 What kind of wood is the best to use to make totem poles?

_____

3 What three things did early Native Americans use to carve totem poles?

_____

4 Why were some totem poles placed on the beach?

_____

_____

5 What do some modern carvers use to make totem poles?

_____

6 What two types of organizations are keeping the art of totem poles alive today?

_____

_____

Secret Message

Follow the directions to cross out words in the list below. The leftover words will form a sentence. Write the sentence on the lines.

Clue 1
Cross out all words that begin with the letter B.

Clue 2
Cross out all words that end with the letters ING.

Clue 3
Cross out all words that are colors.

Clue 4
Cross out all words that rhyme with three.

Clue 5
Cross out all 2-letter words.

SEWING BIRD RED EUROPEAN KNEE TO EXPLORERS AT BEAR
SEE WERE PURPLE AMAZED BINGO GREEN IS WHEN SING
FREE THEY YELLOW FIRST DO BROTHER RING SAW ME TOTEM
BIKE OF POLES TREE COMING TWO ORANGE ON HUNDRED
BOX WHITE PARKING YEARS BOY PINK AGO STRING

_____

_____

_____

U.S. Facts & Fun • EMC 6306 • ©2005 by Evan-Moor Corp.

Find the Hidden Fish

Can you find seven fish hidden in this picture? Circle them. Then color the picture.

The fish look like this:

"I Have a Dream"— Martin Luther King, Jr.

When Martin Luther King, Jr., was growing up, black Americans were not treated the same as white Americans. In the southern part of the United States, they could not eat at restaurants with white people. They could not swim in the same pools or drink from the same water fountains. Schools for black children were not as good as schools for white children.

Martin wanted to change all that. He gave speeches and led marches. These speeches and marches showed the world that black Americans should be treated the same as white Americans.

Martin especially wanted to make the world a better place for his children. One day, his daughter asked to go to an amusement park called Funtown. Martin cried and told her that only white people were welcome at Funtown. A few years later, Funtown opened to all children. Martin said that the day he took his daughter to the park was one of the happiest days of his life.

In 1963, Martin gave a speech in front of 250,000 people in Washington, D.C. He told them, "I have a dream." Martin's dream was that one day his children would not be judged by their skin color. Martin's work helped make that dream possible.

Show What You Know!

Write whether each statement is *true* or *false.*

1 During Martin's life, black Americans and white Americans were always treated equally.   _____

2 Black children and white children went to different schools.   _____

3 Martin wanted to make the world a better place for his children.   _____

4 Martin gave many speeches during his life.   _____

5 Martin never took his daughter to Funtown.   _____

6 Martin gave his "I have a dream" speech in 1959.   _____

7 Only a few people heard Martin's "I have a dream" speech.   _____

8 Martin helped make things better for black Americans.   _____

It may be hard to believe today, but during Martin's life many places were segregated. This means that black people and white people were separated. Unscramble each word below to find some places that were segregated. The clues will help you.

1. UTASERTRNA

___ ___ ___ ___ ___ ___ ___ ___ ___ ___

CLUE a place to eat

2. OSHOLC

___ ___ ___ ___ ___ ___

CLUE a place of learning

3. EVIMO   HAETRET

___ ___ ___ ___ ___

___ ___ ___ ___ ___ ___ ___

CLUE a place to see a film

4. USB

___ ___ ___

CLUE you ride on this to go places

5. OPOL

___ ___ ___ ___

CLUE a great place to cool off

6. EHTOL

___ ___ ___ ___ ___

CLUE where you might stay on vacation

U.S. Facts & Fun • EMC 6306 • ©2005 by Evan-Moor Corp.

Martin's Maze

These people want to hear Martin's "I have a dream" speech. Help them find their way to the gathering.

A Hidden Railroad

It is the 1850s. Imagine you are a runaway slave in the southern part of the United States. You know that if you get to Canada, you will be safe. But Canada is hundreds of miles away. How will you find your way?

For many slaves, the answer was the Underground Railroad. This "railroad" was actually a network of people all over the United States. These people were called conductors. They led slaves from one "station," or hiding place, to another.

Harriet Tubman was a slave who escaped with help from the Underground Railroad. After she won her freedom, she went back to the South. She led about 300 slaves to freedom.

Many stations on the Underground Railroad were houses or barns. These stations often had clever hiding places. Slaves gathered in secret rooms. They hid behind fake walls or under false floors. When night fell, a conductor led them from their hiding places to the next station.

Working on the Underground Railroad was dangerous for both escaped slaves and conductors. They could be fined, arrested, or even killed. However, they continued their work to bring freedom to thousands of men, women, and children.

U.S. Facts & Fun • EMC 6306 • ©2005 by Evan-Moor Corp.

Show What You Know!

Write the word that matches each definition. The letters in the shaded boxes spell the answer to the question.

1. people who are not free
   ▨ __ __ __ __ __

2. last name of a famous slave
   ▨ __ b __ __ __

3. to charge with a crime
   ▨ __ c __ __ s __

4. top part of a house
   ▨ __ __ __ __

5. opposite of *north*
   ▨ __ __ __ __

What did slaves use to find their way at night?

Answer: The __ __ __ __ __

---

1. a unit of measurement
   ▨ __ __ l __

2. many times
   ▨ f __ __ __

3. something few people know
   ▨ __ __ __ __ __

4. to run away
   ▨ s __ __ p __

5. a place where passengers catch trains
   ▨ __ __ __ __ __ __

What was Harriet Tubman's nickname?

Answer: __ __ __ __ __

Help This Runaway

Help this runaway find his way to the next station. Work each math problem and write the answer on the line. Then write the answers in the boxes next to the landmarks on the map on page 41. Draw a trail from the smallest number to the largest number to find the way.

1. $126 - 17 =$ _____ **big rock**

2. $96 + 78 =$ _____ **cave**

3. $15 \times 3 =$ _____ **pine trees**

4. $11 \times 12 =$ _____ **old shack**

5. $96 - 78 =$ _____ **pond**

6. $35 + 46 =$ _____ **apple tree**

U.S. Facts & Fun • EMC 6306 • ©2005 by Evan-Moor Corp.

Loving Lincoln

In 1915, the land along the western bank of the Potomac River in Washington, D.C., was an empty marsh. Today, it is the site of a magnificent memorial to the 16th president of the United States, Abraham Lincoln.

The Lincoln Memorial is a large building lined with 36 columns. Inside the memorial is a huge statue of Lincoln sitting in a chair. He looks serious and sad.

A sculptor named Daniel Chester French designed Lincoln's statue. The marble statue is 19 feet tall and weighs 175 tons. The statue is so large that it could not be built all at once. Instead, a company in New York City built the statue in 28 sections. Each section was sent to Washington. Finally, the whole statue was put together like a giant puzzle.

The monument is built of stone from many different parts of the United States. Words from some of Lincoln's most famous speeches are carved on the walls.

The Lincoln Memorial was completed in 1922. A large crowd of 50,000 people viewed the dedication. Since then, millions more have visited this special place that honors a great president.

There are quite a few numbers in the article about the Lincoln Memorial. Match each number to the statement that describes it.

28   the height of Lincoln's statue in feet

50,000   the weight of the statue in tons

16   the number of columns in the building

19   the number of people who attended
                                              the dedication of the memorial

36   the number of sections in which
                                              the statue was made

175   the number of Lincoln's presidency

CHALLENGE

Write some things you know about Abraham Lincoln. Why do you think he was honored with a memorial?

_____

_____

_____

_____

Lincoln Kriss-Kross

Fill in the blanks with words from the story to complete each sentence below. Then fit each word into the puzzle grid on page 45. We've put in the first letter of each word to get you started.

1. The Lincoln Memorial is located along the Potomac ___ ___ ___ ___ ___.

2. The land where the memorial was built was once a wet ___ ___ ___ ___ ___.

3. The Lincoln Memorial has 36 ___ ___ ___ ___ ___ ___ ___.

4. The memorial shows Lincoln sitting in a huge ___ ___ ___ ___ ___.

5. The sculptor's last name was ___ ___ ___ ___ ___ ___.

6. Putting the statue together was like making a giant ___ ___ ___ ___ ___ ___.

7. Words from some of Lincoln's famous ___ ___ ___ ___ ___ ___ ___ are carved on the walls of the memorial.

U.S. Facts & Fun • EMC 6306 • ©2005 by Evan-Moor Corp.

Scrambled Words

Unscramble each word below. A clue is given for each word to help you figure it out.

ESNPIRDET _____   the leader of a country

RCUOSPLT _____   someone who designs a statue

NECOSIT _____   a smaller part of a whole thing

AMELMIRO _____   a building or statue that honors someone who has died

BEARLM _____   what Lincoln's statue is made of

The Streets of NEW YORK

New York is a big city. It is packed with people, places, and things to see. How do people get around New York? By rail and roads, water and air, and even underground!

Most of New York's streets are arranged in a grid. Numbered streets run east and west. Numbered and named avenues run north and south. This system makes it easy to get around. There are about 12,000 taxis in the city. Other people take buses to get around the crowded streets. There are more than 200 bus routes in the city.

New York's underground subway system began in 1904. Today, there are about 469 subway stations. These subway trains zip passengers underneath the city's streets. Some trains even travel through tunnels underneath rivers! Other aboveground trains take passengers in and out of the city. Grand Central Station has 123 train lines!

New York's harbor is full of boats. Special ferries take passengers around the water. The Staten Island Ferry runs 24 hours a day. Cruise ships also sail into New York Harbor from other parts of the world.

New York City has two large airports. They are the John F. Kennedy and La Guardia Airports. So no matter where you want to go, you can get there from New York!

U.S. Facts & Fun • EMC 6306 • ©2005 by Evan-Moor Corp.

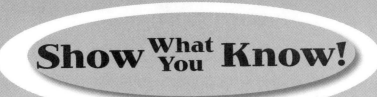

City COUNTDOWN

Match each number or date to the statement that describes it.

1904   taxis in New York

200   train lines at Grand Central Station

2   hours the Staten Island Ferry runs

469   year the first New York subway opened

12,000   New York City airports

123   bus routes

24   subway stations

Getting AROUND TOWN

List all the things mentioned in the article that describe how people travel around New York City. Can you think of some more ways people might travel around the city? List them, too!

_____   _____

_____   _____

_____   _____

Magical MANHATTAN

Much of New York City is on the island of Manhattan. There are lots of famous landmarks there! Using the clues given on page 49, identify each landmark. Then write the correct number in the box beside each picture.

U.S. Facts & Fun • EMC 6306 • ©2005 by Evan-Moor Corp.

CLUES

1. Marble lions "guard" the **New York City Public Library**.

2. A movie ape climbed to the top of the **Empire State Building**.

3. You can ice-skate at **Rockefeller Center** all year round.

4. You'll need to take a boat ride to get to the **Statue of Liberty**.

5. Throughout the years, there have been a number of scams in which people were led to believe they were buying the **Brooklyn Bridge**.

6. The tiered top of the **Chrysler Building** is a New York skyline standout.

7. Flags of many countries fly outside the **United Nations Building**.

8. The **Angel Statue** in Central Park is a famous "photo-op."

CHALLENGE

Look at the pictures for 30 seconds. Then close the book. How many pictures can your remember? Name them.

_____   _____

_____   _____

_____   _____

The Statue of Liberty – Pennies for the Pedestal

In 1865, a group of Frenchmen decided that France should give a gift to the United States to honor the friendship between the two countries. This gift became the Statue of Liberty, which stands in New York Harbor. France would build and pay for the statue. The United States would build and pay for the pedestal, or base.

Few Americans donated money to build the pedestal. By 1885, the statue was completed, but the pedestal was not. Then Joseph Pulitzer got into the act. Pulitzer was the publisher of a New York City newspaper called the *New York World*.

In March 1885, Pulitzer published an editorial in his paper. He said that the rich people in New York should be ashamed of not donating money to the pedestal fund. Instead, he encouraged the "common people" to donate.

Money poured in. In the first week, $2,000 was donated! The *New York World* published the names of everyone who sent a donation. Many donations came from school children. Others came from poor working men and women. One man donated $1 and signed his letter, "Poor but not mean."

By August, the *New York World* announced that $100,000 had been collected. The pedestal was completed 8 months later. The Statue of Liberty finally had a place to stand.

U.S. Facts & Fun • EMC 6306 • ©2005 by Evan-Moor Corp.

Number these events in the order in which they happened.

☐ Joseph Pulitzer asked the "common people" to donate money for the pedestal.

☐ The Statue of Liberty was completed, but had no pedestal.

☐ $2,000 was collected.

☐ The pedestal was completed.

☐ A group of Frenchmen wanted to give a gift to the United States.

☐ The *New York World* collected $100,000 for the pedestal.

☐ The Statue of Liberty was opened to the public.

SECRET STATUE

Use the code below to figure out the name of the man who built the Statue of Liberty.

☆ = A	▭ = F	◖ = O
▲ = B	◆ = G	⚡ = R
⚙ = C	—o = H	▼ = S
↔ = D	◗ = I	○ = T
▢ = E	⬡ = L	⊠ = U

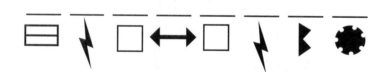

Mixed-Up Liberty

The Statue of Liberty has gotten very mixed up! Find six things wrong with this picture. Write them on the lines.

1 _____

2 _____

3 _____

4 _____

5 _____

6 _____

HONORING OUR FIRST PRESIDENT

George Washington was the first president of the United States. Many places in the U.S. have been named after him. There are cities, counties, mountains, and even a state named Washington. But the most inspiring tribute to George Washington is the Washington Monument.

The Washington Monument is located on the Mall in Washington, D.C. (another place named after George!). Congress wanted to honor Washington with a monument even before he died in 1799. In 1783, Congress agreed to build a statue of Washington on horseback in the capital. This statue, however, was never built.

As the years passed, people wanted something fancier to honor the nation's first president. A design contest was held in 1836. The final design was chosen in 1845. The monument would be a marble obelisk. An obelisk is a tall four-sided structure that is narrower at the top than it is at the bottom.

The Washington Monument was finished in 1885. It opened to the public three years later. The monument can be seen from all over the city. More than a million people visit the monument every year. It is one of the most popular sites in the U.S. capital.

U.S. Facts & Fun • EMC 6306 • ©2005 by Evan-Moor Corp.

Draw a line to match each event to the date when it occurred.

The monument opens to the public.   1845

Washington dies.   1888

The design contest is held.   1783

Congress agrees to build a
statue of Washington.   1799

The monument is finished.   1836

The winning design is chosen.   1885

BY THE NUMBERS

The Washington Monument is:
- 10 times taller than it is wide
- 35 square feet wide at the top
- 55 square feet wide at the base
- 555 feet high

It has:
- 192 memorial stones inside
- 897 steps from top to bottom

WASHINGTON'S
WORD SEARCH

Circle each of the words listed below in this puzzle. Be sure to look across, up and down, diagonally, and backward.

```
O D Z A S R P S H U G D P E S K E J L U G N E
G B Z C Y U C I R S E P D R P E H W T L Y L R
X X E W I D E T O M O N O Z E L E H A L A Q X
L M V L M T N E X D R E X M Y S H T I T O K W
M O F J I L Y K P S G K A L O E I E I R U S B
E N V O E S T A T U E Q C R P P H D C B N M G
Y U W G D H K M T A U A B T A N A L E N N A O
P M I E V M J A N I R J V C R C T I V N F Z K
Z E X D I C L F N T E U R V E T C Y U X T K L
N N H B S M D M A L L I O S F B E H Y U P M R
G T A G I H K O P I J L N H O H E T H A T S H
J O U N T Z S L C N A E O R A L U P O P S C J
H T M A R B L E A M D P H J M I E N A J O T Y
D E S I G N K N O D V W U N C H L S A U I N V
```

OBELISK   MALL

SITE   DESIGN

MARBLE   PRESIDENT

HONOR   POPULAR

CITY   CAPITAL

MONUMENT   STATUE

VISIT   GEORGE

MONUMENT MAZE

Can you find your way through the maze inside the Washington Monument? Collect the letters along the way to spell the last name of the original designer of the monument, Robert Mills. You may <u>not</u> backtrack or touch any other letters.

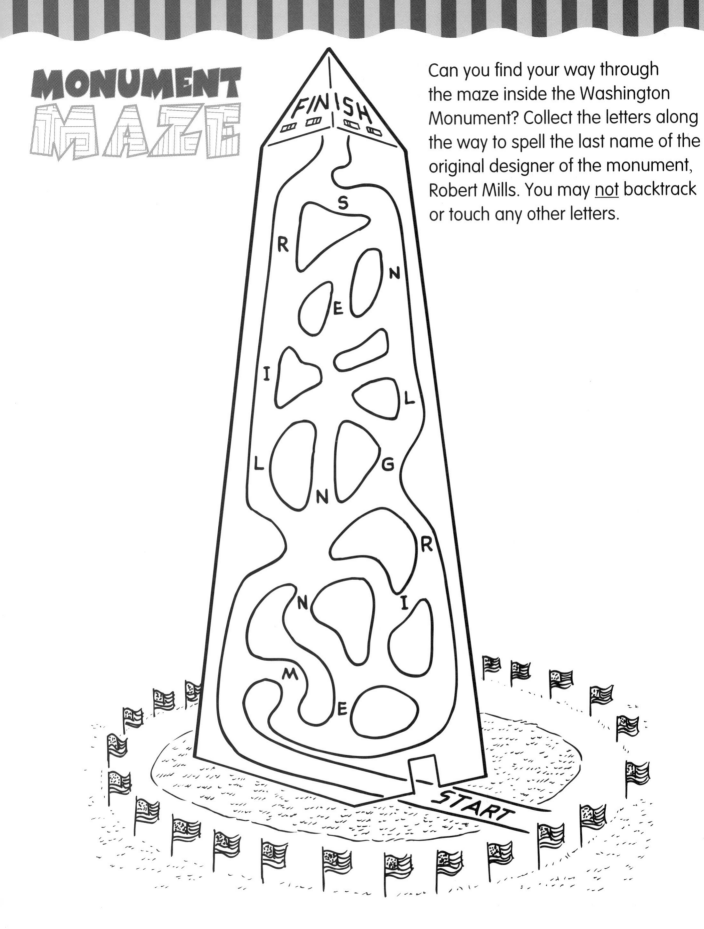

The designer's name was Robert ___ ___ ___ ___ ___.

Norman Rockwell—
The People's Painter

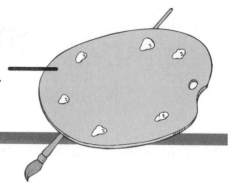

If you lived in Arlington, Vermont, or Stockbridge, Massachusetts, during the 1940s and 1950s, you might have appeared in a famous painting. American artist Norman Rockwell lived in those towns. He liked to use neighbors as models for his artwork.

Norman was born in 1894. He always liked to draw. When Norman grew up, he painted covers for magazines. Many of these covers showed regular people doing ordinary things. But Norman's talent made these scenes magical.

Many of Norman's magazine covers included children. He showed boys and girls playing sports, teasing each other, or going to school. The people in his paintings were not beautiful or glamorous. They were just average Americans. People recognized themselves in these scenes and enjoyed them.

Norman often asked neighbors to pose for his paintings. For one magazine cover, Norman showed two boys dressed in baseball uniforms. They are laughing at a third boy, who is pushing his sister in a baby carriage. A boy named Billy was the model for all three boys.

Norman died in 1978. Today, his paintings hang in museums all over America. His work is a tribute to Americans and their lives.

Fill in the blanks to complete each sentence below.

1 Norman Rockwell was a famous American _____ .

2 Norman painted many _____ covers.

3 Norman liked to paint _____ Americans.

4 Norman often asked his _____ to pose for his pictures.

5 Norman lived in the states of _____ and _____ .

6 Today, Norman's paintings hang in _____ all over America.

5 Fun Facts About Norman Rockwell

- When he was growing up, Norman's favorite author was Charles Dickens.

- Norman had such pale skin, his mother called him "Snow-in-the-Face."

- Norman delivered mail to earn money for art lessons.

- Norman painted more pictures of Abraham Lincoln than any other president.

- Norman's covers for *The Saturday Evening Post* were so popular that the magazine printed 250,000 extra copies every time his art was on the cover.

Create-a-Picture

Norman Rockwell painted more pictures of Abraham Lincoln than any other president. You can draw your own picture of Lincoln. Copy each square from the grid on page 60 into the same place on this grid to create your picture. Then color the picture.

1	2	3	4	5	6	7
8	9	10	11	12	13	14
15	16	17	18	19	20	21
22	23	24	25	26	27	28
29	30	31	32	33	34	35
36	37	38	39	40	41	42
43	44	45	46	47	48	49

AMERICA'S HORSE

There are many kinds of horses in America, but the Morgan horse is truly an American horse. All Morgan horses are descended from one stallion that lived in Vermont during the late 1700s. This horse was named Justin Morgan, and he gave his name to a whole new breed.

Justin Morgan was born around 1790 on a farm in Massachusetts. His original name was Figure. Figure's owner didn't think much of the colt. So he gave him to his cousin, Justin Morgan, to pay a debt. Morgan took the horse home to his Vermont farm. Later, the horse would become known by his owner's name.

Figure was small, but he was tough! Morgan entered Figure in pulling contests. The horse pulled heavy logs and won lots of prizes. Later, Figure became a racehorse. He won every race he entered.

Figure wasn't just strong and fast. He was also friendly and handsome. He had a smooth, shiny coat and a gentle personality. Soon Figure was famous all over Vermont and Massachusetts. People started calling him Justin Morgan, after his owner. The little horse lived until 1821, when he was about 30 years old.

Justin Morgan was the father of many horses. These horses looked and acted much like him. They became a whole new breed called the Morgan horse. Today, it is one of the most popular breeds in America.

U.S. Facts & Fun • EMC 6306 • ©2005 by Evan-Moor Corp.

Write whether each statement is *true* or *false*.

1 _____ Figure was a big strong horse.

2 _____ Figure was born around 1700.

3 _____ Figure's original owner gave him to a cousin to repay a debt.

4 _____ Figure won many log-pulling contests.

5 _____ Figure lost a lot of races.

6 _____ The Morgan horse started in Europe.

7 _____ During his life, Figure was not famous.

8 _____ Figure lived to be about 30 years old.

9 _____ The Morgan horse continues to be popular today.

WORD SCRAMBLES

Reread paragraphs three and four of the story. Underline the words that describe Figure, the first Morgan horse. Then write the words below.

_____   _____

_____   _____

_____   _____

_____

Use the words you wrote to unscramble the words below.

LFIEYRDN   _____

ETEGNL   _____

LSALM   _____

NRSOGT   _____

DAHOEMSN   _____

TAFS   _____

UMASFO   _____

U.S. Facts & Fun • EMC 6306 • ©2005 by Evan-Moor Corp.

A Different Horse

Can you find and circle the one horse that is not the same as the others? On the lines, write a sentence that tells what makes this horse different.

The Liberty Bell—
Let Freedom Ring

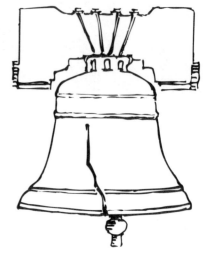

In 1751, the people of Philadelphia decided their city needed a bell. The bell was ordered from a factory in London. The bell makers were told to write "Proclaim liberty throughout all the land unto all the inhabitants thereof" on the side of the bell.

The new bell arrived in Philadelphia in September 1752. But the first time the bell was rung, it cracked! Two men offered to make a new bell in Philadelphia. They melted down the bell and added copper to make it stronger. The new bell worked, but it sounded awful. So the bell was melted down again. This time, tin was added to the mixture. In June 1753, the bell was finally fixed.

On July 8, 1776, the Liberty Bell rang at the first reading of the Declaration of Independence. Exactly 59 years later, the Liberty Bell cracked again when it was rung to announce the death of John Marshall, Chief Justice of the Supreme Court. It was repaired, but cracked again in 1846.

The Liberty Bell would never ring again. However, it could still make sound when it was tapped gently. In 1915, the bell's chime was carried over wires from Philadelphia to San Francisco in the first coast-to-coast telephone call. In 1926, it was tapped again to celebrate 150 years of independence. During World War II, it announced the American invasion of Europe. And every July 4, the bell is tapped to once more "proclaim liberty throughout all the land."

Show What You Know!

Number the following events in order from the event that happened first to the event that happened last.

_____ The Liberty Bell cracked when rung to announce the death of John Marshall.

_____ The bell arrived in Philadelphia from London.

_____ The Liberty Bell's chime was carried across the country in the first coast-to-coast telephone call.

_____ The bell was melted down and copper was added.

_____ A bell was ordered from England.

_____ The bell was rung to announce the signing of the Declaration of Independence.

_____ The bell cracked for the first time.

_____ Tin was added to make the bell sound better.

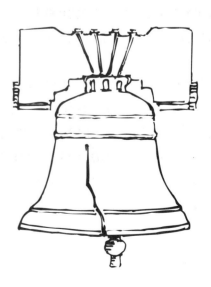

Liberty Bell Word Games

Word Squares

Each bell contains an 8-letter word from the story. Find each word by starting at one of the letters and reading either clockwise or counterclockwise. Then write the words on the lines.

Bell 1: R E G N O R T S

Bell 2: M I A L C O R P

Bell 3: R E P A I R D E

Bell 4: U O N A E C N N

Bell 5: R A M L L A H S

Bell 6: I O N N I V A S

Word Search

How many times can you find the word *bell* in the word search?

I found *bell* _____ times.

```
E E B L E B B B E L B E L
L L L E B L E L L E B E
B L E L L E L L E E E B
L B E B E L L B L L L E
E L L E B E B L E B L L
B L E L E B E E E L E B
B E L L E L B E L L E E
E B E L L L E B B B L E L
E E L B L L L L L E B L
L E B L E B L E L B E L
B E L L B E L E E B L E
B L B E E L L E B E L L
```

Spell It Out

Read about the place where the Liberty Bell was displayed for many years. Cross out every third letter to uncover the name. Write the answer on the line.

I N E D E Y P E W N D P E N F C E E H A X L L O

_____

This building could well be called the birthplace of the United States. It was here that the Declaration of Independence was adopted in 1776 and the Constitution was written and signed in 1787.

Our Nation's
CAPITAL

After the United States won its independence from Great Britain, it faced another problem. What would be the nation's capital city? Between 1776 and 1790, eight cities served as the nation's capital. Now it was time to pick a permanent spot.

President George Washington picked the new capital. He chose a spot that was partly in Maryland and partly in Virginia. This spot was in the middle of the 13 colonies, so it would be a good meeting place for people from all over the country. Maryland and Virginia donated land to create a new area called the District of Columbia. The city itself was named after George Washington.

Washington asked a Frenchmen named Pierre L'Enfant to design the city. L'Enfant planned a city with wide streets and a long mall, or shaded walkway, in the middle. There would be lots of parks and open spaces, too.

Work began on the capital in 1790. It was supposed to be finished by 1800, but it wasn't. John Adams was president in 1800. He didn't care if the city was finished. He moved his family into the White House. Congress didn't care either. They met in Washington for the first time in November 1800.

Over the years, Washington, D.C., has grown bigger and better. The capital has a lot more than government buildings! There are many monuments to American presidents. Other monuments honor soldiers and important people. The city also has dozens of museums. In Washington, D.C., there is a lot to see!

U.S. Facts & Fun • EMC 6306 • ©2005 by Evan-Moor Corp.

Answer the questions.

1 Who picked the site for the new U.S. capital?

_____

2 Why was the site picked?

_____

_____

3 Who designed the nation's capital?

_____

4 What three things did the design include?

_____

_____

_____

5 In what year did John Adams move into the White House?

_____

6 Who is the capital named after?

_____

7 What does the "D.C." in "Washington, D.C." stand for?

_____

8 What three groups are honored with monuments in our nation's capital?

_____

_____

_____

A Visit to WASHINGTON, D.C.

Put on your walking shoes! Today, you're going to stroll through Washington, D.C. and visit some of the many famous landmarks—monuments, museums, and famous government buildings located there. Use the landmarks map on page 73 to complete the questions.

1 The Ellipse is an oval-shaped open area. It is located between which two famous

landmarks? _____   _____

2 The highest court in the nation is located in Washington, D.C. What is its name?

_____

What major government building is it located behind? _____

3 Which memorial on the map honors war veterans?

_____

4 Name the long, narrow open area where many museums are located.

_____

5 If you visit the National Archives, you can see the original Declaration of
Independence, the Constitution, and the Bill of Rights. What number is the

National Archives on the map? _____

Is it north or south of the National Mall? _____

6 The memorial to Thomas Jefferson, third president of the U.S., is located near
three bodies of water. Name them.

_____   _____

_____

U.S. Facts & Fun • EMC 6306 • ©2005 by Evan-Moor Corp.

7 If you stood on the steps of the Capitol Building and looked down the mall, you would see structures honoring which two presidents? Name them.

_____   _____

8 Which of the museums would be your first choice to visit? Name it and circle it

on the map. _____

Tell why you would choose to go there. _____

_____

_____

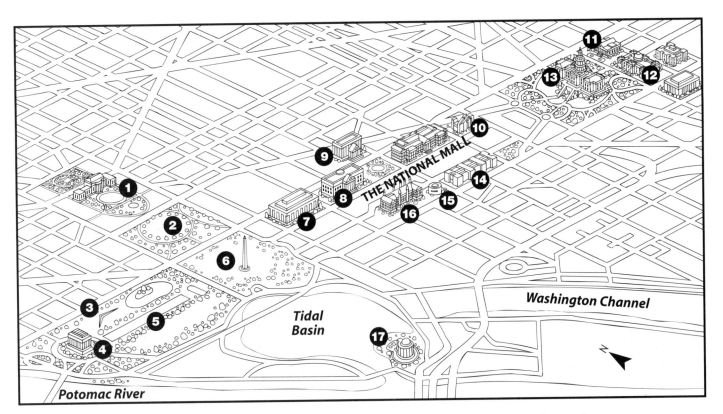

1. White House
2. The Ellipse
3. Vietnam Veterans Memorial
4. Lincoln Memorial
5. Reflecting Pool
6. Washington Monument
7. National Museum of American History
8. National Museum of Natural History
9. National Archives

10. National Gallery of Art
11. Supreme Court
12. Library of Congress
13. U.S. Capitol
14. National Air and Space Museum
15. Hirshhorn Museum
16. Smithsonian Institution
17. Jefferson Memorial

GOLD!

On a cold winter's day in January 1848, James Marshall was walking along the American River in California. Marshall was building a sawmill for a man named John Sutter.

Marshall saw something shiny in the water. He scooped it up. The object looked like a gold nugget. Marshall brought the nugget back to Sutter, and the two men tested it. It was gold!

Sutter wanted to keep the discovery a secret. He wanted to protect his property. He needed time to make sure he could claim the gold for himself.

The discovery of gold, however, was too big a secret to keep. Within a few weeks, word got out that there was gold at Sutter's Mill. Gold fever swept the nation. Men rushed to California from all over the United States and the world to prospect for gold. They dreamed of incredible riches.

The most popular way to find gold was panning. A gold prospector scooped up river water in a pan and swirled it around. Heavy gold would settle on the bottom. It was rare, however, to find enough gold to make a fortune. Most gold prospectors did not get rich, but many stayed in California.

As for John Sutter, he lost all his land to prospectors. He lost his fortune, too. James Marshall's discovery did not make him rich either, but their names live on in an exciting part of American history.

U.S. Facts & Fun • EMC 6306 • ©2005 by Evan-Moor Corp.

Match each word from the story to its definition.

prospector	land owned by someone
panning	a place that saws logs into boards
fortune	say something belongs to you
nugget	a method of finding gold in water
sawmill	a small chunk or lump
discovery	unusual
property	a large sum of money
claim	sank
rare	someone hunting for gold
settled	something that is found

GOLD RUSH

Players:
2 or more

You need:
- one coin
- a marker for each player

How to Play:
1. Decide on the order of play.
2. Players flip the coin to see how many spaces to move.
   heads—move 1 space forward
   tails—move 2 spaces forward
3. Then follow the directions on each square.
4. The first player to reach the finish line is the winner!

When Ah strike Gold, Ah'm gonna git me a team o' horses!

Ah'm gonna git me a mansion fit fer a king!

Ah'm gonna git a big screen Plasma TV... if anybody ever invents one!!

TO THEM THAR HILLS

U.S. Facts & Fun • EMC 6306 • ©2005 by Evan-Moor Corp.

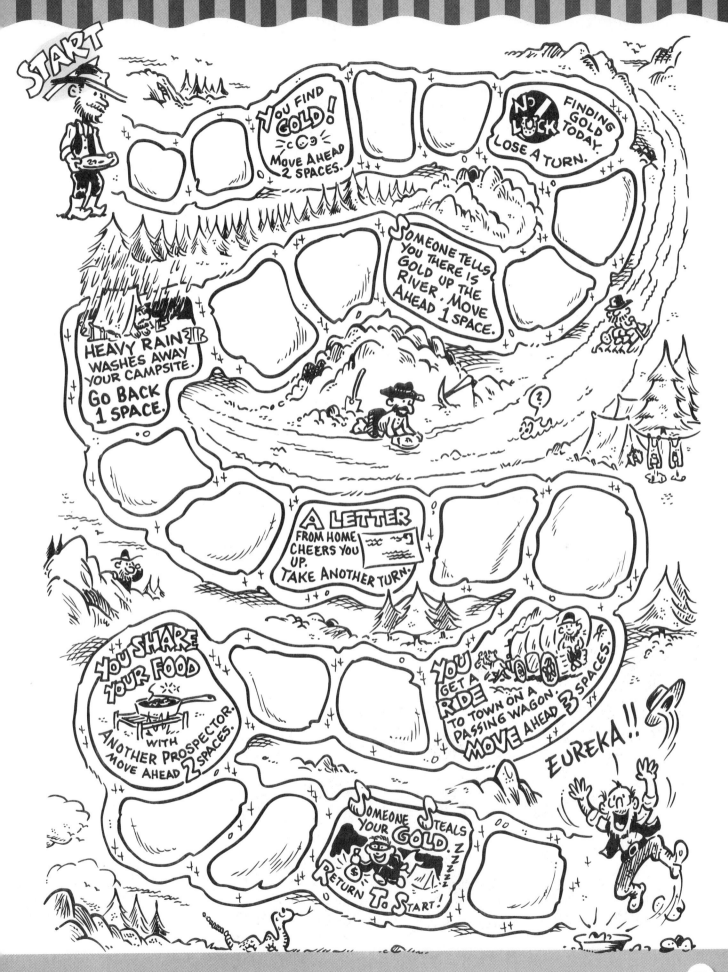

Lewis & Clark —
The Great Explorers

In 1803, the United States was much smaller than today. Everything west of the Mississippi River was a wilderness. In 1803, President Thomas Jefferson bought the Louisiana Territory from France. The "Louisiana Purchase" doubled the size of the United States.

Jefferson hired Meriwether Lewis and William Clark to explore the new territory. Lewis and Clark left St. Louis, Missouri, in May 1804 with 50 men. The group was called the Corps of Discovery.

Lewis and Clark were very brave men. There were no maps to show them where they were going. They didn't know what they would find in the woods and deserts of the West. Every day brought new dangers. Sometimes they met unfriendly natives. At other times, they lost their food and supplies.

The explorers traveled up the Missouri River to Fort Mandan in what is now North Dakota. They spent the winter there. In April 1805, they headed west. A Native American girl named Sacagawea went with them. Sacagawea talked to Native Americans the group met and helped Lewis and Clark find their way.

Lewis and Clark reached the Pacific Ocean on November 18, 1805. They spent the winter in what is now Oregon. Then they headed back home. When they returned to St. Louis in September 1806, there was a great celebration. Lewis and Clark had been gone for more than 2 years. They had traveled more than 7,600 miles.

Lewis and Clark wrote stories and drew pictures of everything they saw on their trip. They described the people they met and the animals they found. The men brought back samples of plants and made maps. Their journey helped Americans discover their new land.

U.S. Facts & Fun • EMC 6306 • ©2005 by Evan-Moor Corp.

Number the following events in the order in which they happened.

[ ] Lewis and Clark reached North Dakota.

[ ] Lewis and Clark spent the winter in Oregon.

[ ] President Jefferson bought the Louisiana Territory from France.

[ ] Lewis and Clark reached the Pacific Ocean.

[ ] Lewis and Clark left St. Louis.

[ ] The United States was a much smaller country.

[ ] Sacagawea joined Lewis and Clark.

[ ] Jefferson hired Lewis and Clark to explore the new territory.

[ ] Lewis and Clark returned to St. Louis.

Westward Journey

Use the map of Lewis and Clark's journey on page 81 to answer these questions.

1 Is it farther from St. Louis to Fort Mandan or from Fort Mandan to Great Falls?

_____

2 Where do the Missouri River and the Mississippi River meet?

_____

3 What is directly south of Fort Mandan?

_____

4 If you wanted to get to Great Falls from Fort Mandan, in which direction would you travel?

_____

5 Which is farther west, the Snake River or the Columbia River?

_____

6 What place was located at the western end of Lewis and Clark's journey?

_____

7 What town is about halfway between St. Louis and the Arikara villages?

_____

8 What river runs from Fort Mandan south to St. Louis?

_____

U.S. Facts & Fun • EMC 6306 • ©2005 by Evan-Moor Corp.

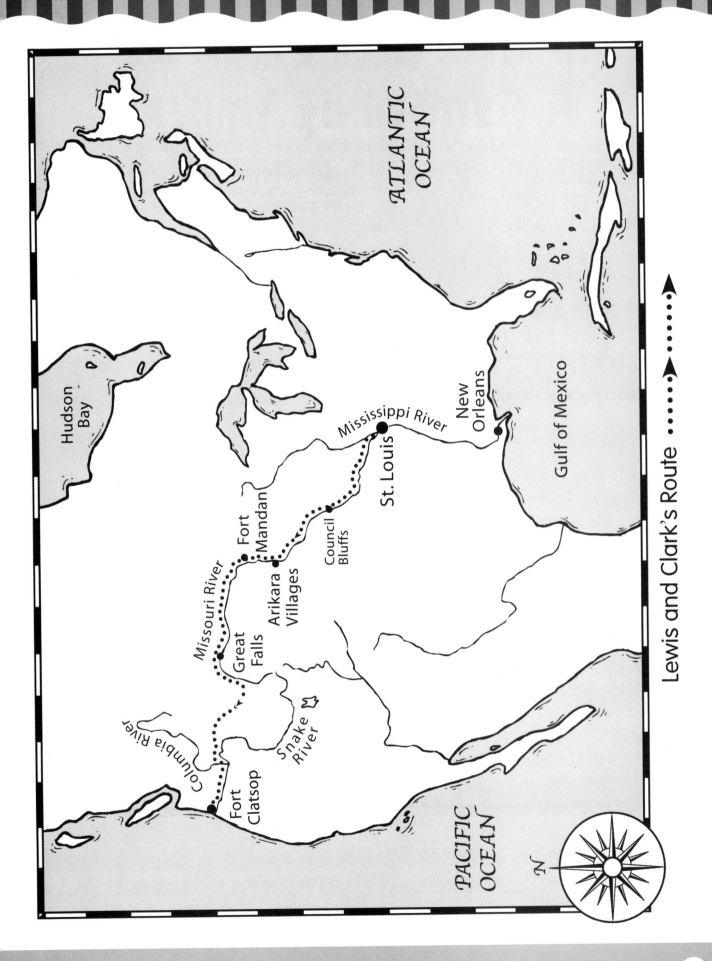

Lewis and Clark's Route ••••••►

The Bald Eagle — A Symbol of America

The men who founded the United States had lots of decisions to make. One of them was what the new country's national emblem should be. Many people thought the bald eagle was a good choice. One man, Benjamin Franklin, disagreed. He said that eagles were already symbols for many other countries. He felt the United States should do something different. Franklin also thought eagles were bad examples because they stole food from other birds.

Franklin wanted the turkey to be the national symbol. He called the turkey a respectable bird. It was also native to America. And, as far as anyone knew, it had never been the emblem of any nation!

The U.S. Congress argued about the emblem for six years. Finally, in 1782, they chose the bald eagle. The bald eagle lives only in North America. It also represents freedom, strength, and courage. These were all qualities that Congress wanted the new nation to have. Somehow, the turkey just didn't inspire the same feelings!

During the 20th century, the bald eagle became endangered. Many of the birds were poisoned by a chemical called DDT. Things are looking up, however, for this mighty bird. DDT is no longer used in the United States. Today, the bald eagle can once again be seen flying over the land it represents.

Use information from the story to fill in the blank in each sentence below.

1. Many people wanted the _____ to be the national emblem of the United States.

2. Benjamin Franklin thought the _____ should be the emblem.

3. Franklin said that the turkey was a _____ bird.

4. Franklin didn't like eagles because they _____ food from other birds.

5. Congress argued about the emblem for _____ years.

6. Congress chose the eagle because it represents freedom, strength,

   and _____ .

7. During the 20th century, eagles became _____ .

8. A chemical called _____ poisoned many bald eagles.

9. Today, the bald eagle still _____ in the United States.

The bald eagle is the central figure on the Seal of the President of the United States.

Word Stairs

Fit the following words from the story into the puzzle below. We've filled in the first word to get you started.

FRANKLIN
FREEDOM
TURKEY
EAGLE
EMBLEM
NATIVE
ENDANGERED
EXAMPLES
CENTURY
CONGRESS
DDT

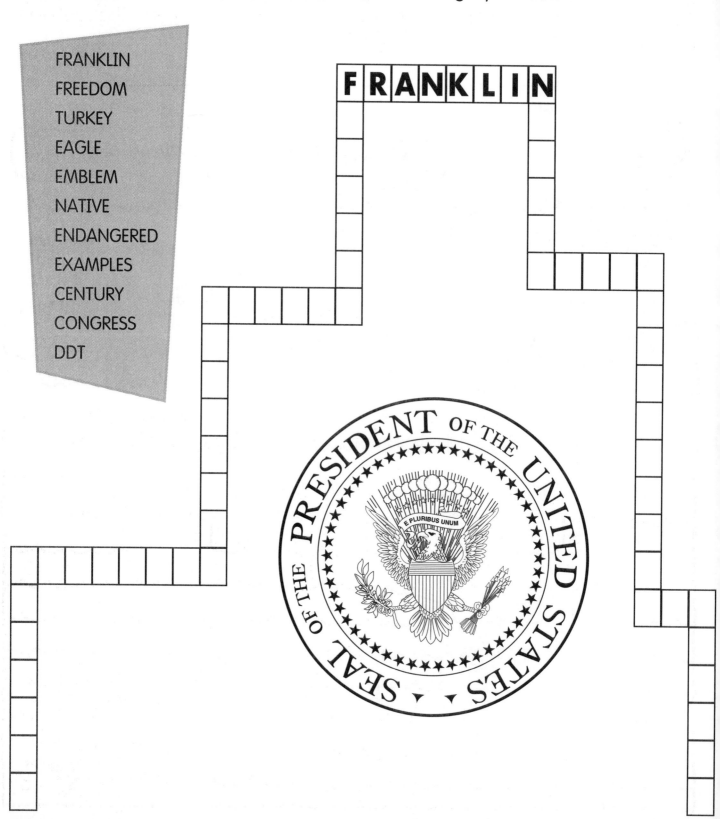

FRANKLIN

U.S. Facts & Fun • EMC 6306 • ©2005 by Evan-Moor Corp.

Gone Fishin'

An eagle's sharp eyesight lets it see fish swimming in rivers far below. Help this eagle find a salmon for dinner.

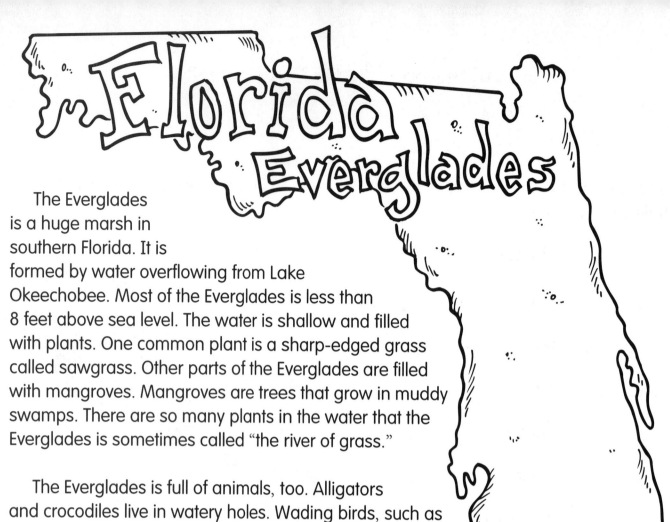

Florida Everglades

The Everglades is a huge marsh in southern Florida. It is formed by water overflowing from Lake Okeechobee. Most of the Everglades is less than 8 feet above sea level. The water is shallow and filled with plants. One common plant is a sharp-edged grass called sawgrass. Other parts of the Everglades are filled with mangroves. Mangroves are trees that grow in muddy swamps. There are so many plants in the water that the Everglades is sometimes called "the river of grass."

The Everglades is full of animals, too. Alligators and crocodiles live in watery holes. Wading birds, such as egrets and anhingas, walk through the water looking for fish. Bald eagles fly overhead. Bobcats, panthers, and bears prowl along the shore. The waters and swamps are filled with snakes and fish. A large, gentle mammal called the manatee also lives and swims in the water.

Over the years, people have done a lot of damage to the Everglades. Lake Okeechobee has been dammed many times, so less fresh water reaches the Everglades. People have also drained swamps to provide land for new houses and businesses. Because of these events, many animals in the Everglades are at risk.

The good news is that the Everglades is now a national park, so the land cannot be developed or changed. Endangered animals are also protected by the government. These efforts may help save one of America's national treasures.

U.S. Facts & Fun • EMC 6306 • ©2005 by Evan-Moor Corp.

Show What You Know!

Write *yes* next to the animals that the story says live in the Everglades. Write *no* next to the animals that don't live there.

_____	alligator	_____	snake
_____	woodchuck	_____	kangaroo
_____	bald eagle	_____	horse
_____	bear	_____	egret
_____	penguin	_____	bobcat
_____	anhinga	_____	camel
_____	manatee	_____	tiger
_____	panther	_____	crocodile

Look at the animals that you wrote *yes* beside. Then write each animal's name in the group to which it belongs.

 Reptiles    **Birds**    **Mammals**

_____   _____   _____

_____   _____   _____

_____   _____   _____

_____   _____   _____

EVERGLADES SCRAMBLE

Unscramble the words below and write them on the lines. Then unscramble the shaded letters to find out a way to travel through the Everglades.

HINT: The number after each scrambled word tells you the paragraph where the word can be found.

A B T O C B (2) ☐ ___ ___ ___ ___ ___

A F I R L O D (1) ___ ___ ☐ ___ ___ ___ ___

G A N I W D (2) ___ ___ ___ ☐ ___ ___

E A D M A G (3) ___ ☐ ___ ___ ___ ___

A K P R (4) ___ ___ ☐ ___

N E N R E E D A G D (4) ___ ___ ___ ☐ ___ ___ ___ ___ ___ ___

E R W T A (1) ___ ___ ☐ ___ ___

Shaded letters: ___ ___ ___ ___ ___ ___ ___

Way to travel: ___ ___ ___   ___ ___ ___ ___

HINT: what you breathe   HINT: another word for *ship*

EVERGLADES MIX-UP

Some crazy things have been lost in the Everglades! Find these five items. Color each item when you find it.

bicycle   telephone   book

baseball cap   lamp

CRAZY HORSE

As settlers moved into the western parts of the United States, they were not always fair to the Native Americans who were already living there. Over the years, there were many battles between Native Americans and the United States Army. One of the most famous Native American heroes was Crazy Horse.

Crazy Horse was born in 1841. He was a member of the Sioux tribe. The little boy was quiet and liked to spend time by himself. But when he got older, Crazy Horse became a good fighter and a leader.

In 1866, the U.S. government promised the Sioux that they could have all the land in the Black Hills in South Dakota. This land was holy to the Sioux. But after gold was discovered in the Black Hills, the government broke its promise. It ordered all Sioux people to leave the Black Hills and report to the government.

Crazy Horse was a mighty warrior by then. He told his people to disobey the U.S. order. On June 25, 1876, General George Custer led 600 soldiers against Crazy Horse and the Sioux. Crazy Horse and 1,000 Sioux warriors defeated the U.S. Army and killed Custer.

Crazy Horse's victory did not last long. In 1877, he surrendered. A few months later, he was killed in a fight with a prison guard. Crazy Horse's parents claimed his body and took it away. No one knows where Crazy Horse is buried, but his story lives on today.

U.S. Facts & Fun • EMC 6306 • ©2005 by Evan-Moor Corp.

Show What You Know!

Complete the crossword puzzle using words from the story.

Across

4. Crazy Horse led many ___ ___ ___ ___ ___ ___ ___ ___ into battle.

5. The U.S. government promised the Sioux that they could have the

   Black ___ ___ ___ ___ ___ .

6. Crazy Horse was a member of the ___ ___ ___ ___ ___ tribe.

Down

1. Crazy Horse defeated General George ___ ___ ___ ___ ___ ___ .

2. The U.S. Army and the Native Americans fought

   many ___ ___ ___ ___ ___ ___ ___ .

3. The U.S. broke its promise when

   ___ ___ ___ ___ was discovered
   in South Dakota.

5. Crazy Horse was a famous
   Native American

   ___ ___ ___ ___ .

WARRIOR MAZE

This Native American warrior wants to join Crazy Horse. Can you help him find his way through the maze?

U.S. Facts & Fun • EMC 6306 • ©2005 by Evan-Moor Corp.

SECRET SYMBOLS

Each symbol below stands for a different letter. Can you figure out the code to learn the name of the battle between Crazy Horse and General Custer?

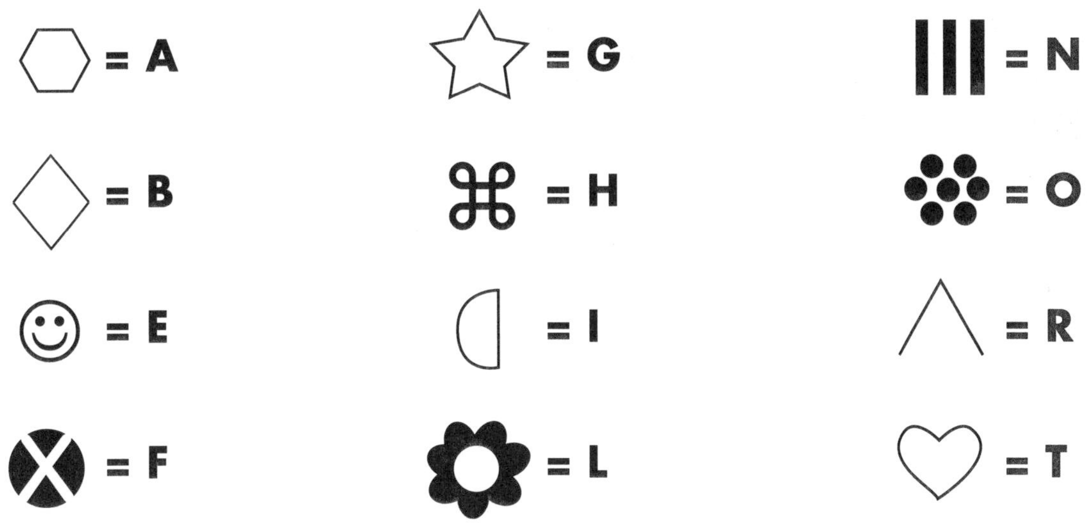

⬡ = A ☆ = G ||| = N

◇ = B ⌘ = H ❀(o) = O

☺ = E ◗ = I ∧ = R

⊗ = F ✿ = L ♡ = T

___ ___ ___   ___ ___ ___ ___ ___ ___
♡ ⌘ ☺   ◇ ⬡ ♡ ♡ ✿ ☺

___ ___   ___ ___ ___   ___ ___ ___ ___ ___ ___
❀ ⊗   ♡ ⌘ ☺   ✿ ◗ ♡ ♡ ✿ ☺

___ ___ ___ ___ ___ ___ ___
◇ ◗ ☆ ⌘ ❀ ∧ |||

GETTYSBURG —
Civil War Battlefield

During Abraham Lincoln's presidency, southern states wanted to leave the U.S. and form a new country. Northern states and President Lincoln said, "No!" The Civil War, which lasted from 1861 to 1865, then began.

The bloodiest battle of the Civil War took place on July 1–4, 1863. The battlefield was near the small town of Gettysburg, Pennsylvania. By the time the shooting stopped, 51,000 soldiers were dead or injured.

After the battle, the people of Gettysburg buried more than 6,000 bodies left on the battlefield. Pennsylvania's governor didn't like how the graves were scattered all over the ground. He wanted a better memorial. A special design was created for the new cemetery on 17 acres on land. The graves were placed in a semicircle around a tall monument.

The cemetery was dedicated on November 19, 1863. President Abraham Lincoln gave a speech called the Gettysburg Address. The speech was only two minutes long, but it was very powerful. Lincoln said that the soldiers had fought and died to preserve freedom. He asked everyone to continue the fight so that the United States would always be free.

Later, the battlefield was added to the cemetery site, and the whole area became a national park. Today, the Gettysburg National Military Park covers more than 2,100 acres. It has more than 900 monuments and 415 cannons. A flame called the Eternal Light Peace Memorial burns night and day as a symbol of hope. More than a million people visit the park every year to remember the dead and learn about the Civil War.

Match each number or date to the statement that describes it.

1863   dead and wounded

2,100   acres in the original cemetery

900   monuments

415   cannons

6,000   year in which the Battle of Gettysburg
                             was fought

2   visitors each year

51,000   bodies left on the
                             battlefield

17   minutes in the
                             Gettysburg Address

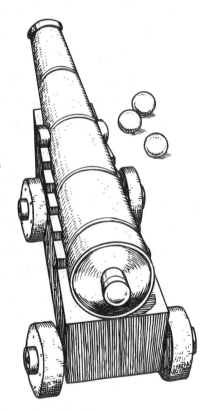

1,000,000   acres in Gettysburg
                             National Military Park

The BLUE and the GRAY

During the American Civil War, the northern states were known as the Union. Union soldiers wore dark blue jackets and either dark blue or sky blue trousers. The Southern states called themselves the "Confederate States of America." Confederate soldiers wore gray uniforms. Color the uniforms appropriately.

U.S. Facts & Fun • EMC 6306 • ©2005 by Evan-Moor Corp.

CANNONS of GETTYSBURG

The Gettysburg National Military Park has a lot of cannons. Look back at the story to find out how many.

There are _____ cannons at Gettysburg National Military Park.

Find and circle the two cannons that are the same.

THE MIGHTY GRIZZLY

The United States is filled with many animals, both large and small. One of the most powerful animals is the grizzly bear.

The grizzly got its name because of the white or silver tips on its dark fur. This lighter-colored fur makes the bear looked "grizzled," or gray. A grizzly bear's fur is very thick. This thick fur protects the bear from cold weather and wet conditions.

Grizzlies can be up to 10 feet tall when they stand on their back legs. A male bear can weigh between 400 and 800 pounds. A grizzly's claws and teeth are big, too! The claws measure about 4 inches long. The teeth are about 3 inches long.

Grizzlies use their sharp claws and teeth when they hunt. These bears will eat almost anything, including small animals, young deer, fish, insects, nuts, berries, and honey. These bears usually live about 18 years, but some can live up to 30 years.

Until the 1700s, grizzlies lived all the way from Mexico into Canada. These bears could be found as far east as Ohio and Kentucky. But as the settlers moved west, they took over the bear's territory. Hunters killed many bears. Today, the grizzly is a threatened species. About 40,000 grizzlies live in Alaska and western Canada. A few hundred live in Montana, Wyoming, Washington, and Idaho. The rest live in zoos, which is the best place for people to see this powerful bear up close.

U.S. Facts & Fun • EMC 6306 • ©2005 by Evan-Moor Corp.

Show What You Know!

Write whether each statement is *true* or *false*.

1 _____ Today, grizzly bears live all over the United States.

2 _____ The grizzly is the largest bear in North America.

3 _____ Grizzlies only eat meat.

4 _____ A grizzly bear's fur is dark with lighter-colored fur on the ends.

5 _____ Grizzlies used to be found in Ohio.

6 _____ Many grizzlies were killed by hunters.

7 _____ Grizzlies have thin fur.

8 _____ Most grizzlies live about 18 years.

9 _____ Grizzlies only weigh about 200 pounds.

10 _____ Grizzlies can be up to 10 feet tall when they stand on their back legs.

Secret Message

Follow the directions to cross out words in the list below. The leftover words will form a sentence. Write it on the lines.

Clue 1
Cross out all words that are numbers.

Clue 2
Cross out all words that end with the letters ED.

Clue 3
Cross out all words that are things to eat.

Clue 4
Cross out all words that rhyme with toy.

Clue 5
Cross out all 4-letter words.

Clue 6
Cross out all words that begin with R.

SIXTEEN   WANTED   THE   ROBOT   CATS   GRIZZLY   PANCAKE   BOY
NINE   IS   JOY   CARD   REALLY   THE   COOKIE   WALKED   STATE   ONE
PIZZA   RING   ANIMAL   BOOK   DESTROY   OF   HOME   PRINTED
ROCKS   CALIFORNIA   SEVEN   SPINACH   AND   NOODLES   PICK
MONTANA   PAINTED   TREE

_____

_____

U.S. Facts & Fun • EMC 6306 • ©2005 by Evan-Moor Corp.

Hidden Grizzlies

Can you find eight grizzly bears hiding in this picture? Color them.

America's Uncle

Have you ever seen a picture of a tall man with a long white beard who wears a red, white, and blue suit? That man is Uncle Sam. He has been a symbol of the United States for almost 200 years.

No one is really sure where Uncle Sam came from. Some people think the first Uncle Sam was a real person named Sam Wilson. Wilson was a butcher. He shipped meat to the American army during the War of 1812. Wilson marked his barrels of meat "U.S." One day, someone asked a worker at Wilson's factory what the "U.S." stood for. The worker replied, "Uncle Sam Wilson." After that, the soldiers started calling the meat "Uncle Sam's meat." They called themselves "Uncle Sam's army."

In the 1830s, people began using Uncle Sam as a cartoon symbol for the United States. These artists gave Uncle Sam his red, white, and blue suit and his top hat.

During World War I, Uncle Sam was used to encourage men to join the army. A poster showed Uncle Sam pointing. The poster read, "I want YOU for the U.S. Army."

Today, Uncle Sam is still a symbol of the United States. You can see him in cartoons, posters, and advertisements. He is one of the most common and easily recognized symbols of America.

Show What You Know!

Answer the questions.

1 What does Uncle Sam wear?

_____

2 How long has Uncle Sam been a symbol of the United States?

_____

3 What job did Sam Wilson have?

_____

4 What did a worker say the "U.S." on Wilson's barrels stood for?

_____

5 When did Uncle Sam appear on a poster to urge men to join the U.S. Army?

_____

6 What did the poster say?

_____

7 What are three things Uncle Sam often appears on?

_____

_____

Name That Symbol

Can you name each of the American symbols pictured below?

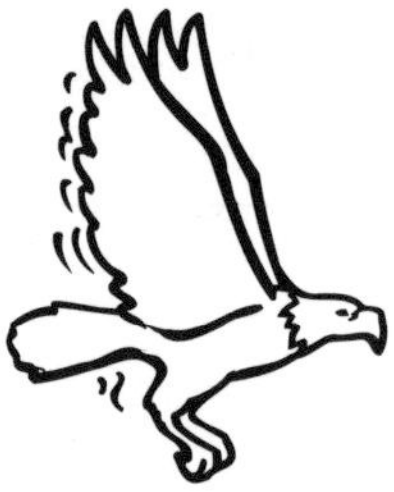

B ___ ___ ___
E ___ ___ ___ ___

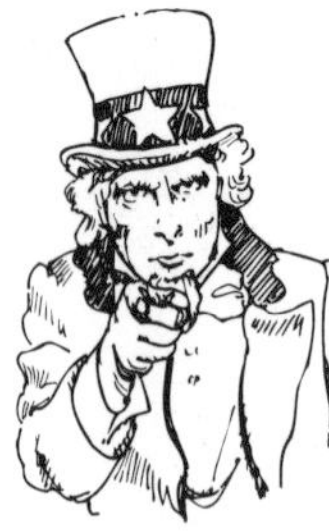

U ___ ___ ___ ___
S ___ ___

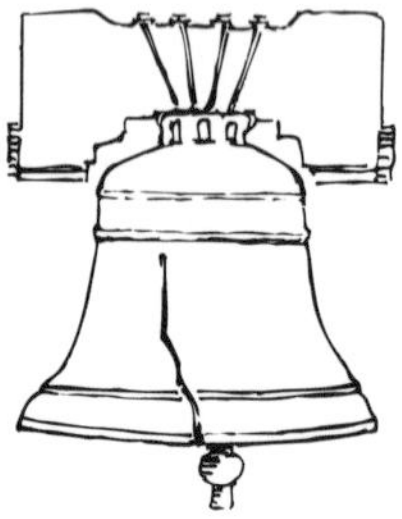

L ___ ___ ___ ___ ___ ___
B ___ ___ ___

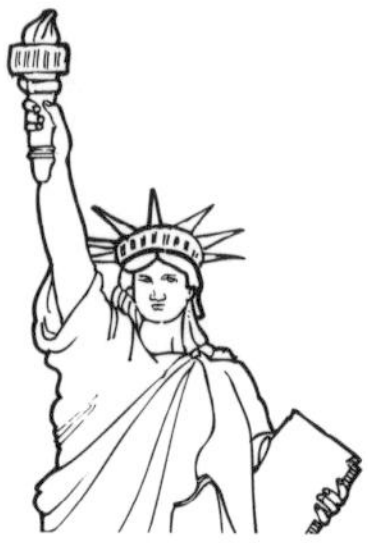

S ___ ___ ___ ___ ___
___ ___
L ___ ___ ___ ___ ___ ___ ___

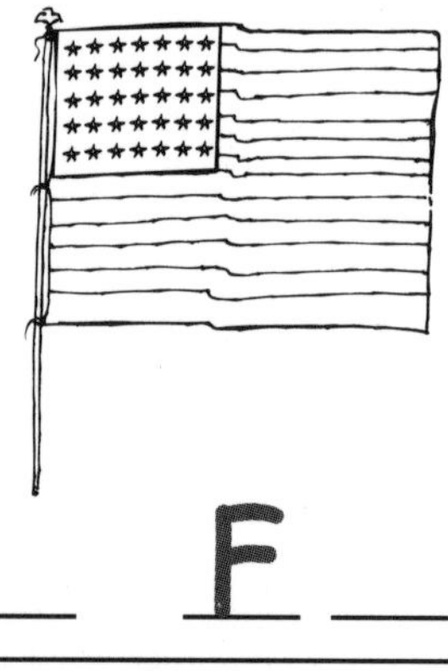

U ___ F ___ ___ ___

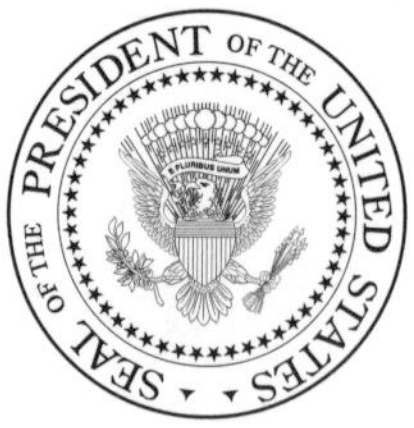

G ___ ___ ___ ___
S ___ ___ ___

CHALLENGE If you had to choose another symbol for the U.S., what would it be? Draw a picture of your choice on the back of this paper.

Math Clues

Solve each math problem below. Then use the answers to figure out the code and discover the name of the man who designed the World War I poster of Uncle Sam.

92 – 48 = _____ = **F**

70 x 4 = _____ = **Y**

43 x 2 = _____ = **L**

65 + 15 = _____ = **J**

73 – 39 = _____ = **E**

34 + 59 = _____ = **M**

9 x 15 = _____ = **S**

85 x 3 = _____ = **T**

16 x 6 = _____ = **N**

98 – 43 = _____ = **G**

54 – 25 = _____ = **A**

89 + 13 = _____ = **O**

87 + 41 = _____ = **R**

 ‾‾‾‾   ‾‾‾‾   ‾‾‾‾   ‾‾‾‾   ‾‾‾‾‾
  80   29   93   34   135

 ‾‾‾‾ ‾‾‾‾ ‾‾‾‾ ‾‾‾‾‾ ‾‾‾‾ ‾‾‾‾‾ ‾‾‾‾ ‾‾‾‾ ‾‾‾‾‾ ‾‾‾‾‾
  93   102   96   255   55   102   93   34   128   280

 ‾‾‾‾   ‾‾‾‾   ‾‾‾‾   ‾‾‾‾   ‾‾‾‾
  44   86   29   55   55

Ellis Island—Entrance to AMERICA

Between 1890 and 1954, millions of people passed through the doors of the immigration station on Ellis Island in New York Harbor. This station was the gateway to America for many poor Europeans looking for a better life.

When they reached Ellis Island, immigrants faced many tests. These tests decided whether the immigrant was healthy and could legally enter the United States. It usually took several hours for each immigrant to be processed. Then they were free to leave the island and start a new life in America.

By 1924, changes in U.S. laws reduced immigration through Ellis Island. In 1954, the station was closed. The abandoned buildings fell into decay.

In 1982, plans were made to restore the island and turn it into a museum. Organizers came up with a special way to raise money. They asked families to contribute $100 to have an immigrant ancestor's name carved on a wall on the island. The project was a success and quickly raised $20 million. The museum opened in 1990.

Today, the Ellis Island Immigration Museum is part of the National Park Service. It is one of the country's most popular historical sites. Visitors can learn about the immigrant experience, look up the records of their ancestors, and retrace their steps as they walk the halls of this fascinating museum and listen to its stories.

Number the following events in the order in which they happened.

☐ Ellis Island fell into decay.

☐ Restoration organizers came up with a special way to raise money.

☐ The Ellis Island Immigration Museum opened.

☐ Changing laws reduced the number of immigrants passing through Ellis Island.

☐ Plans were made to restore the island.

☐ Ellis Island Immigration Station opened.

☐ Ellis Island is one of America's most popular historical sites.

☐ Ellis Island closed.

Word Search

Circle each of the words in the puzzle below. Look in all directions.

```
D P H Z L E G A L M M W E Q
R I T E S T S P Z U U X Y O
E H M T U Y Z M L S J J C D
S B O M C B V Y L E T C L R
T A Y K I S L A D U C V L O
O U S H Y G Y U B M K L A H
R N X C V Y R Z N A Y E W P
E U R O P E Y A E P N R T Y
B V E D Y H Q W N V X D P W
Q R C R E V B Z D T Y O O R
Y Z O V X C P R O C E S S N
G T R O P P A U R T Y L D B
B N D H P S D Y L E C H J X
P I S L A N D R W T H R L U
```

IMMIGRANT	ISLAND	RECORDS	MUSEUM
RESTORE	WALL	ABANDON	DECAY
TESTS	EUROPE	LEGAL	PROCESS

U.S. Facts & Fun • EMC 6306 • ©2005 by Evan-Moor Corp.

The Peopling of AMERICA

The chart below shows the number of immigrants coming to the United States from eight countries during the period of 1880 to 1930. Translate the information in the chart to the graph at the bottom of the page.

Italy	4,600,000
Austro-Hungarian Empire	4,000,000
Russian Empire	3,300,000
German Empire	2,800,000
Great Britain	2,300,000
Canada	2,300,000
Ireland	1,700,000
Sweden	1,100,000

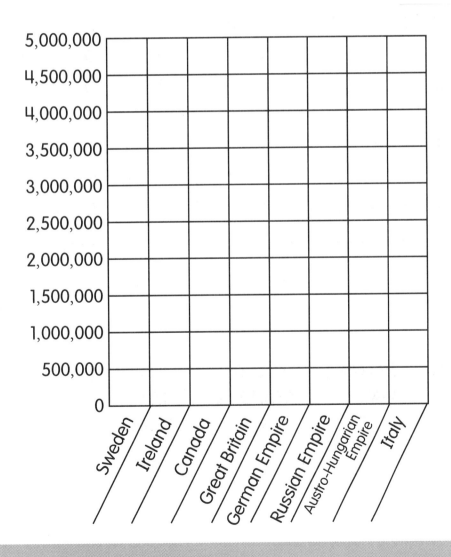

Rosa Parks—
A Seat on the Bus

Can sitting down on a public bus be an act of protest? It was for one black American woman who lived in Montgomery, Alabama, in 1955. At that time, the buses in Montgomery were segregated. Blacks could not sit in the same part of the bus as whites. A black person also had to give up his or her seat if a white person wanted to sit.

On December 1, 1955, Rosa Parks was on her way home from work. When the bus driver asked her to give up her seat for a white man, Rosa said no. She was tired of being pushed around. Rosa was arrested for refusing to get up.

Rosa's friends organized a boycott. They refused to ride the buses until the law was changed. The boycott lasted for 11 months. During that time, black people walked to work and to school. They took cabs and shared rides with friends. They faced a lot of anger and violence from some white people.

On November 13, 1956, the United States Supreme Court said that segregation on the buses was against the law. The boycott had worked! From that day on, blacks and whites had to be treated equally on city buses. This victory led to equal rights in many other areas of American life. Today, Rosa Parks is known as "the mother of the civil rights movement."

Show What You Know!

Fill in the blanks with the word from the story that completes the sentence.

1 Rosa Parks lived in Montgomery, ___ ___ ___ ___ ___ ___ ___ .

2 The buses in Montgomery were

___ ___ ___ ___ ___ ___ ___ ___ ___ ___ ___ .

3 Rosa refused to give up her ___ ___ ___ ___ to a white man.

4 Rosa was ___ ___ ___ ___ ___ ___ ___ ___ for refusing to get up.

5 Rosa's friends organized a bus ___ ___ ___ ___ ___ ___ ___ .

6 Blacks had to walk, share rides, or take ___ ___ ___ ___ .

7 They faced anger and ___ ___ ___ ___ ___ ___ ___ ___ from some
   white people.

8 On November 13, 1956, the ___ ___ ___ ___ ___ ___ ___ Court said
   segregation was against the law.

9 From that day on, blacks and whites had to be treated

___ ___ ___ ___ ___ ___ ___ on city buses.

10 Rosa Parks is called "the ___ ___ ___ ___ ___ ___ of the civil rights
    movement."

Rosa's Crossword

Use the clues to complete the puzzle.

Across

6. to show unwillingness or disapproval
8. the rights of every citizen (2 words)
10. a planned joining with others to refuse to deal with another group

Down

1. kept separate
2. force used to harm
3. something put together in an orderly way
4. having the same rights
5. held by the law
7. a win; defeat of an opponent
9. a place where matters are decided by law

The Bison— Symbol of the West

The Midwest and western parts of the United States were very different 150 years ago. During the 1800s, huge herds of bison roamed the open grasslands and prairies of the West. In 1855, there were more than 75 million bison in the wild. But just 20 years later, there were fewer than 1,000. What happened?

The bison is a large, hoofed mammal. Males can weigh up to 1,800 pounds. They stand about 6 feet tall. Bison have shaggy fur and a hump made of muscle on their backs.

Native Americans used the bison for many things. They ate the meat. The fur was made into blankets. The skin made tipis and clothing. Even the bones could be made into tools.

The Native Americans never killed a lot of bison at one time. But when white settlers moved west, they began slaughtering the bison. Some bison were killed for food. Others were killed to remove them from farmland. Millions more were hunted for sport. A man with a rifle could kill as many as 2,000 bison in one hunting trip.

In the early 1900s, several people decided to save the bison. Small herds were captured and sent to game preserves and zoos. Others were kept safe in national parks. Today, the bison is no longer endangered. But it will never again be able to roam the prairie as it did 150 years ago.

HEY, WHERE DID EVERYBODY GO?

Bison are herbivores. They eat grass and other plant matter.

U.S. Facts & Fun • EMC 6306 • ©2005 by Evan-Moor Corp.

Match each word to the phrase that describes it.

tipi	long-haired
endangered	where bison used to live
slaughter	where most bison live today
rifle	animal that only eats plants
shaggy	Native American home
prairie	large group of animals
game preserve	to kill many animals at the same time
herd	to wander freely
herbivore	gun
roam	in danger of dying out

Baffled Bison

Can you find the two bison that are exactly alike? Draw a circle around them.

U.S. Facts & Fun • EMC 6306 • ©2005 by Evan-Moor Corp.

Back to the Herd

This bison has become separated from the herd. As you find the correct path through the maze, you will spell out another name that bison are sometimes called. Write the name on the line.

_____ _____ _____ _____ _____ _____

Colonial Williamsburg

Imagine being able to walk the streets of a colonial town and see how people lived hundreds of years ago. That was the dream of Dr. William Goodwin. In 1934, his plan to make Williamsburg, Virginia, into a living history museum came true.

Williamsburg was the capital of the Virginia colony during the early 1700s. It was a living place, filled with stores, workplaces, and churches. Children played, did chores, and went to school.

Richmond became Virginia's capital in 1780. After that, Williamsburg became less lively and popular. By 1926, many of its buildings were in ruins.

Dr. Goodwin was a minister in Williamsburg. He and his friends wanted to restore the city. They hired scientists called archaeologists to find out what Williamsburg looked like 200 years earlier. Then they collected money, bought land, and restored buildings. In 1934, colonial Williamsburg opened to the public.

Today, thousands of visitors stroll Williamsburg's streets. They see people in colonial dress acting out scenes from life in old Williamsburg. They watch a blacksmith make nails and see children roll hoops down the street. They listen in on a meeting about whether Virginia should declare its independence from England. They learn how wigs were made and see horses parade in the streets. They visit the houses of the rich and the poor and see how different people lived.

Colonial Williamsburg is a living history lesson and a fun way to visit the past.

Show What You Know!

Write whether each statement is *true* or *false*.

1 _____ Williamsburg was once the capital of the Virginia colony.

2 _____ In 1785, the capital was changed to Richmond.

3 _____ Dr. William Goodwin was a minister in the 1700s.

4 _____ Goodwin wanted to restore Williamsburg.

5 _____ Goodwin did not need any help to restore the city.

6 _____ Archaeologists are scientists who study the past.

7 _____ Colonial Williamsburg opened to the public in 1934.

8 _____ Visitors can see many things in Williamsburg.

9 _____ Only rich people lived in Williamsburg.

Colonial Trades _____

People of many trades worked in colonial Williamsburg. Match each trade with its description. You may need to use a dictionary.

cooper	melted brass and bronze and molded them into many items
milliner	ground grain into flour
apothecary	sold fabric and made cloth items
founder	made barrels and other wooden containers
miller	made medicines and acted as a doctor

Fancy Dress
Kriss-Kross

At night, rich residents of colonial Williamsburg often attended fancy parties called balls. Below is a list of some of the clothes they wore. Can you fit each word into the grid below?

HINT: Start with the categories that have only one answer.

3- letter word
WIG

4- letter words
COAT
GOWN

5- letter words
CUFFS
SHOES

6- letter words
GLOVES
TIGHTS

8- letter word
BRITCHES

9- letter word
PETTICOAT

U.S. Facts & Fun • EMC 6306 • ©2005 by Evan-Moor Corp.

Digging for History

Archaeologists found many old items when they dug into Williamsburg's past. Find the eight items hidden in the bottom of this old well. Color them.

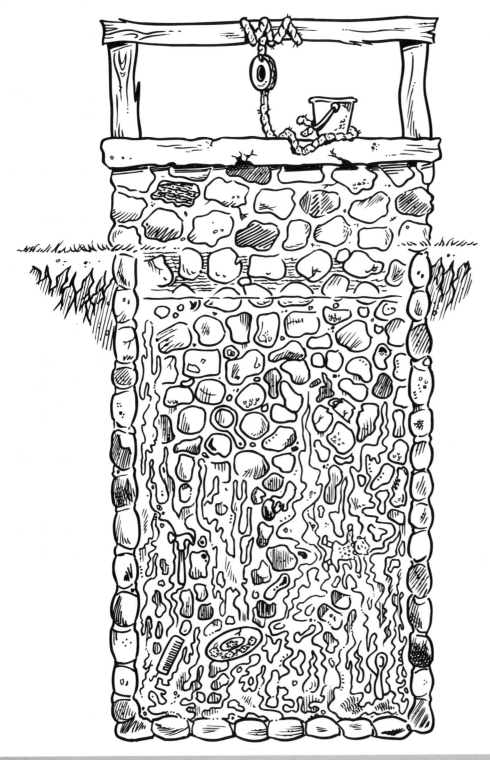

hammer

plate

comb

shoe

spoon

mirror

doll

tea cup

The Wright Brothers
THE FIRST FLIGHT

A cold, windy beach does not seem like a place where history could be made. But that's exactly what happened on December 17, 1903. On that date, two brothers stepped on the sand at Kitty Hawk, North Carolina, and flew into history.

Wilbur Wright was born in 1867. His brother Orville was born in 1871. The brothers lived in Dayton, Ohio. When they were young, the boys liked to build flying machines out of paper, cork, and springs. When the brothers grew up, they still dreamed of flying.

The Wright brothers built several gliders. These planes did not have motors. Instead, they used air currents to lift them into the air and carry them along. The wings of the brothers' gliders were curved. This shape forced air under the wings to lift the plane off the ground.

In 1902, the Wrights added a propeller and an engine to a glider. They called their plane the *Wright Flyer*. In 1903, they went to Kitty Hawk to test their new plane. They chose Kitty Hawk because it was a very windy place. It also had a lot of sand to provide a soft landing spot.

On the morning of December 17, Orville climbed into the plane. The engine roared, and the plane moved forward. Then it lifted into the air! The plane flew about 10 feet off the ground for 12 seconds. This short flight was the beginning of the age of aviation.

Show What You Know!

Write whether each statement is *true* or *false*.

1 _____ The Wright brothers made the first flight at Kitty Hawk, North Carolina.

2 _____ The Wright brothers liked to invent flying toys when they were young.

3 _____ Gliders are planes with motors.

4 _____ A plane's wings are curved.

5 _____ The Wright brothers built only one glider.

6 _____ The Wright brothers added a propeller and motor to a glider to create an airplane.

7 _____ The brothers tested their plane in Dayton, Ohio.

8 _____ Kitty Hawk was a windy, sandy place.

9 _____ Wilbur flew the first airplane.

10 _____ The first flight lasted several minutes.

Airplane Word Search

Circle each word from the story. You'll find them vertically, horizontally, diagonally, or backward.

AVIATION
MACHINE
PROPELLER

CURRENT
GLIDER
CURVED

WINGS
MOTOR
BEACH
WINDY

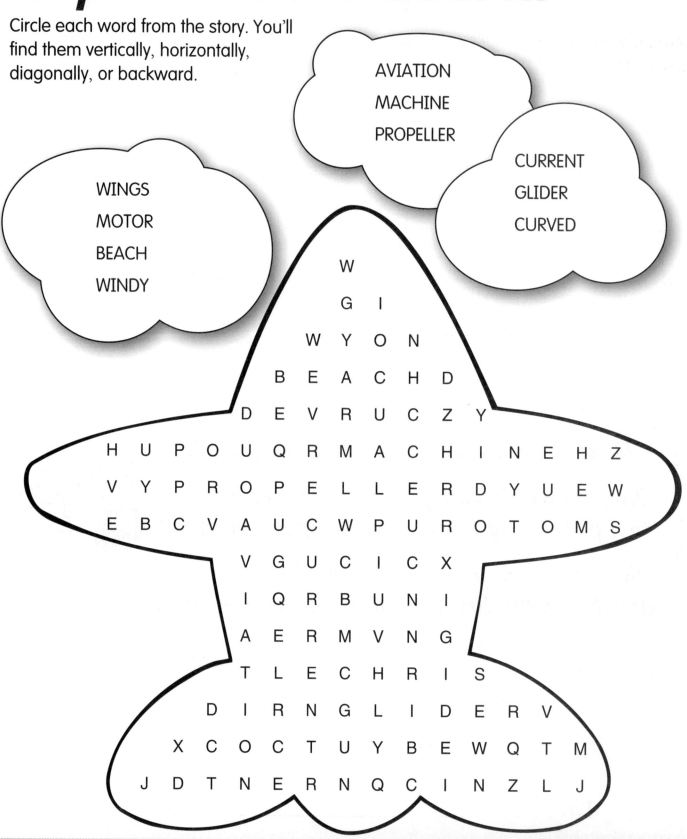

W
G   I
W   Y   O   N
B   E   A   C   H   D
D   E   V   R   U   C   Z   Y
H   U   P   O   U   Q   R   M   A   C   H   I   N   E   H   Z
V   Y   P   R   O   P   E   L   L   E   R   D   Y   U   E   W
E   B   C   V   A   U   C   W   P   U   R   O   T   O   M   S
V   G   U   C   I   C   X
I   Q   R   B   U   N   I
A   E   R   M   V   N   G
T   L   E   C   H   R   I   S
D   I   R   N   G   L   I   D   E   R   V
X   C   O   C   T   U   Y   B   E   W   Q   T   M
J   D   T   N   E   R   N   Q   C   I   N   Z   L   J

U.S. Facts & Fun • EMC 6306 • ©2005 by Evan-Moor Corp.

Airplane

How many words can you make out of the letters in AIRPLANE? Write as many as you can think of on the lines below.

_____   _____   _____   _____

_____   _____   _____   _____

_____   _____   _____   _____

_____   _____   _____   _____

_____   _____   _____   _____

Make 8 words and you're an Orville Wright.

Make 15 words and you're a Chuck Yeager, the first pilot to fly faster than the speed of sound.

Make 20 or more words and you're a Neil Armstrong, the first person to step on the moon.

My score ☐

I'm a _____ .

Franklin Delano Roosevelt— President in a Wheelchair

In 1932, Franklin Delano Roosevelt became the 32nd president of the United States. Just 11 years earlier, becoming president seemed impossible. In 1921, Roosevelt was struck with a disease called polio. The disease left him unable to walk.

Roosevelt worked hard to get his strength back. He refused to feel sorry for himself. In 1924, Roosevelt made an important speech at the convention of the Democratic Party. He surprised everyone by walking across the stage in heavy steel braces. The audience cheered for more than an hour after he finished.

Roosevelt also worked hard to continue his career as a politician. He was elected president in 1932 and served until he died in 1945. He probably would not have been elected if people had known that he was paralyzed.

How did Roosevelt keep his secret? Photographers were not allowed to take any pictures of Roosevelt in a wheelchair. For public appearances, Roosevelt hid his braces under long pants. He walked with a cane or holding someone's arm. Roosevelt's wife, Eleanor, also helped by making public appearances in place of her husband.

Roosevelt led America through the Great Depression of the 1930s and World War II during the 1940s. His spirit and courage helped America through some of the darkest days in the nation's history. That courage helped Roosevelt through his own dark days as well.

Match each event to the year in which it occurred.

Roosevelt is elected president for the first time.   1940s

Roosevelt dies.   1921

World War II occurred.   1932

Roosevelt became ill with polio.   1930s

The Great Depression occurred.   1945

Roosevelt makes a speech at the Democratic convention.   1924

When elected, the president of the United States serves for a 4-year term. Using the information in the story, what term was Roosevelt serving when he died? _____

Word Star

The answer to each clue is a word from the story that begins with the letter *p*. Fit each answer into the star, using the given number of letters to help you. Hint: Three words are written backwards.

5 letters
A disease that paralyzes muscles

6 letters
The people or the community

8 letters
To make something unable to move

9 letters
The leader of the USA

10 letters
A person who runs for government office

12 letters
Someone who takes pictures

Visit the White House

Here is a map of the rooms on the state floor of the White House that are open to the public.

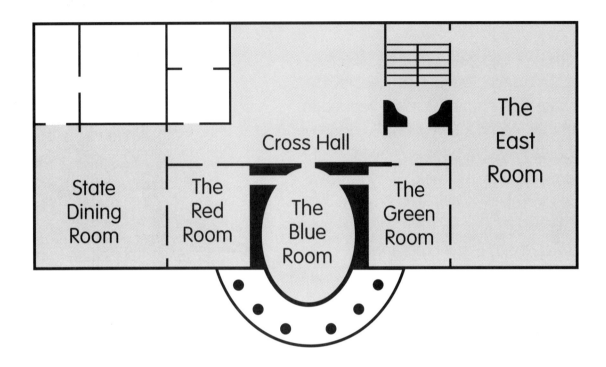

Write the name of the location for each clue below.

1. Portraits of recent presidents are displayed in this thoroughfare. _____

2. This room can seat 140 for dinner. _____

3. First ladies like this room for small receptions and teas. _____

4. This is one of the three oval rooms that George Washington wanted. _____

5. This room, where presidential news conferences are held, is the largest. _____

6. Important visitors are photographed in this room where the walls are covered with mossy-colored silk. _____

Linking East and West—
Building the Railroads

Today, we can get from the eastern part of the United States to the western part in just a few hours. But 150 years ago, this trip took months by covered wagon or horseback. As more people moved west, it became clear that a better way to travel was needed.

In 1862, the U.S. government decided that a transcontinental railroad would run from Omaha, Nebraska, to Sacramento, California. The Central Pacific Railroad would start in California and lay tracks heading east. The Union Pacific Railroad would start in Nebraska and head west.

More than 20,000 men built the transcontinental railroad. Many of them were immigrants from China, Ireland, Germany, and Czechoslovakia. They worked under very hard conditions. They faced the hot desert sun, attacks from Native Americans, avalanches and heavy snow in the mountains, and accidental explosions of the dynamite used to blast through rocks. Thousands of workers lost their lives on the railroad.

After six years of hard work, the Union Pacific and Central Pacific tracks met at Promontory Point, Utah, on May 10, 1869. A golden spike and a great celebration marked the spot.

For the first time, a traveler could journey from the East Coast to the West Coast in a few days. The transcontinental railroad opened the West to millions of Americans and changed the face of the nation forever.

U.S. Facts & Fun • EMC 6306 • ©2005 by Evan-Moor Corp.

Show What You Know!

Answer each question below with information from the story.

1 How did most people travel west before the transcontinental railroad was built?

_____

2 Which two companies were chosen to build the transcontinental railroad?

_____

3 What two cities were the starting points of the railroad?

_____

4 About how many men built the railroad?

_____

5 What four countries provided many of the workers?

_____

_____

6 What were five dangers that the workers faced?

_____

_____

7 Where did the two railroads finally meet?

_____

_____

8 How long did it take to build the transcontinental railroad?

_____

Hidden Words

Starting with the first letter, cross out every other letter to find out the following:

1 a way many people crossed the United States before the transcontinental railroad was built,

X C H O Y V W E A R B E C D P W Y A E G X O M N

— — — — — — — — — — —

2 what the four businessmen who formed the Central Pacific Railroad were called, and

Y T P H R E T B W I Z G A F E O T U O R

— — — — — — — — — —

3 the name of one of these four businessmen who drove the golden spike at Promontory Point, Utah, and also founded a famous university in California.

S L A E P L V A R N O D   M S O T C A W N Y F F O B R K D

— — — — — — — — — — —

Railroad Maze

Can you help the Central Pacific and the Union Pacific meet? Each railroad needs to get through the maze and meet at Promontory Point.

PROMONTORY POINT

Yosemite National Park

Do you like big trees and even bigger rocks? Then pay a visit to Yosemite National Park! This park is full of huge natural wonders.

Yosemite is in California. The park covers more than 1,100 acres of mountains and valleys. It is filled with forests, meadows, streams, and other natural places. Yosemite is in a valley surrounded by the Sierra Nevada Mountain Range.

One of the largest things to see at Yosemite is the giant sequoia trees. These trees are the largest living things in the world. A sequoia can grow up to 300 feet tall and be 35 feet around. Some of these amazing trees are almost 3,000 years old.

Yosemite is also home to many animals. Some animals that live there are bighorn sheep, coyotes, and black bears. You can also find snakes, lizards, fish, and owls.

At one time, only Native Americans lived in Yosemite. Then white settlers moved into the area. They killed many of the native people. They also killed animals and destroyed the land.

A man named John Muir wanted to save Yosemite. He and other people worked very hard to keep the area a special place. Finally, Yosemite became a national park in 1890. That means the land, animals, and plants there are protected by the government.

Millions of people visit Yosemite every year. They come to camp, fish, hike, ski, and take part in other activities. Yosemite National Park is one of America's most popular places.

U.S. Facts & Fun • EMC 6306 • ©2005 by Evan-Moor Corp.

Use information from the story to complete each sentence.

1 Yosemite National Park is full of _____ wonders.

2 Yosemite is in the _____ _____ Mountain Range.

3 A man named _____ _____ helped preserve Yosemite.

4 The _____ tree is the largest living thing in the world.

5 These trees can be more than _____ feet tall.

6 _____ sheep and black _____ live in Yosemite.

7 Long ago, the only people who lived in Yosemite were _____

_____ .

8 Yosemite became a national park in _____ .

9 The park covers more than _____ acres.

10 _____ of people visit
Yosemite every year.

Secret Message

Use the code below to discover an important message about visiting Yosemite National Park.

Z = A   S = H   I = R   V = E   K = P

Y = B   O = L   H = S   L = O

W = D   M = N   G = T   U = F

K O V Z H V   W L   M L G

U V V W   G S V   Y V Z I H

KEEP YOUR FOOD AWAY FROM ME...DON'T WANT IT...WOULDN'T TOUCH IT... I'M ON A DIET...

PLEASE DON'T FEED THE BEARS!

PAINT

Bonus

On the back of this paper, create your own code. Write a message that gives a reason for the message above.

U.S. Facts & Fun • EMC 6306 • ©2005 by Evan-Moor Corp.

Places Around

Yosemite

Find all of the beautiful sites around Yosemite. Color in the squares.

V	F	I	T	O	N	U	R	E	K	A	B	R	D	L	O	M	P
T	E	S	M	H	O	H	A	K	R	M	E	I	G	T	H	C	T
R	B	R	I	D	A	L	V	E	I	L	F	A	L	L	S	S	U
K	G	H	R	I	L	T	R	V	E	Z	P	E	A	S	W	M	O
C	C	Y	R	W	Q	X	O	N	L	G	J	P	C	X	E	H	L
V	F	J	O	H	N	M	U	I	R	T	R	A	I	L	T	I	U
F	A	E	R	S	Z	A	J	O	U	L	Y	S	E	E	W	R	M
I	B	L	L	P	I	R	T	R	P	E	L	N	R	T	D	J	N
L	R	I	A	C	T	I	M	V	E	L	I	H	P	I	S	O	E
O	I	M	K	O	G	P	V	H	A	L	F	D	O	M	E	K	M
R	V	O	E	D	R	O	E	F	Q	Y	C	L	I	E	C	A	E
M	A	I	J	U	A	S	L	J	U	T	G	U	N	S	I	R	A
U	L	X	M	R	I	A	P	E	M	U	R	P	T	O	E	E	D
R	S	N	Y	P	N	G	H	V	K	O	S	S	U	Y	P	Y	O
R	Q	T	T	R	E	R	F	F	R	I	L	Q	U	O	P	V	W
E	U	R	E	T	U	O	L	U	M	N	E	M	E	A	D	W	S
A	T	V	W	K	I	V	E	L	N	S	X	C	H	A	Y	R	L
K	I	R	O	O	C	E	A	K	U	D	V	E	D	T	R	B	J

Bridalveil Falls

Glacier Point

Half Dome

John Muir Trail

Mariposa Grove

Mirror Lake

Sequoia

Tuolumne Meadows

Vernal Falls

Yosemite

One Giant Leap — Landing on the Moon

People have always dreamed of exploring other worlds. For three Americans, that dream came true in July 1969.

America's space program began during the 1960s. The National Aeronautics and Space Administration (NASA) was in charge. Between 1962 and 1966, NASA sent 16 rockets into space. Then, in 1968, three astronauts orbited the moon for the first time on a spacecraft called *Apollo 8*.

On July 16, 1969, NASA launched *Apollo 11*. Onboard were Neil Armstrong, Edwin Aldrin, Jr., and Michael Collins. Their destination was the moon!

On July 19, Armstrong and Aldrin got into a smaller craft called the *Eagle*. Collins stayed onboard the main spacecraft, which was called *Columbia*. A little while later, Armstrong landed the *Eagle* on the moon's surface. Then Armstrong stepped out of the spacecraft and became the first person to stand on the moon. "That's one small step for man, one giant leap for mankind," Armstrong said. About 20 minutes later, Aldrin became the second man on the moon. After planting a flag and doing some experiments, Aldrin and Armstrong returned to *Columbia* and headed back to Earth.

NASA sent six more crews into space before the moon program ended in 1972. Five of those crews landed on the moon. Since then, many men and women have taken different journeys into space. Their journeys started with those historic footsteps more than 30 years ago.

Show What You Know!

Match each number or date to its definition.

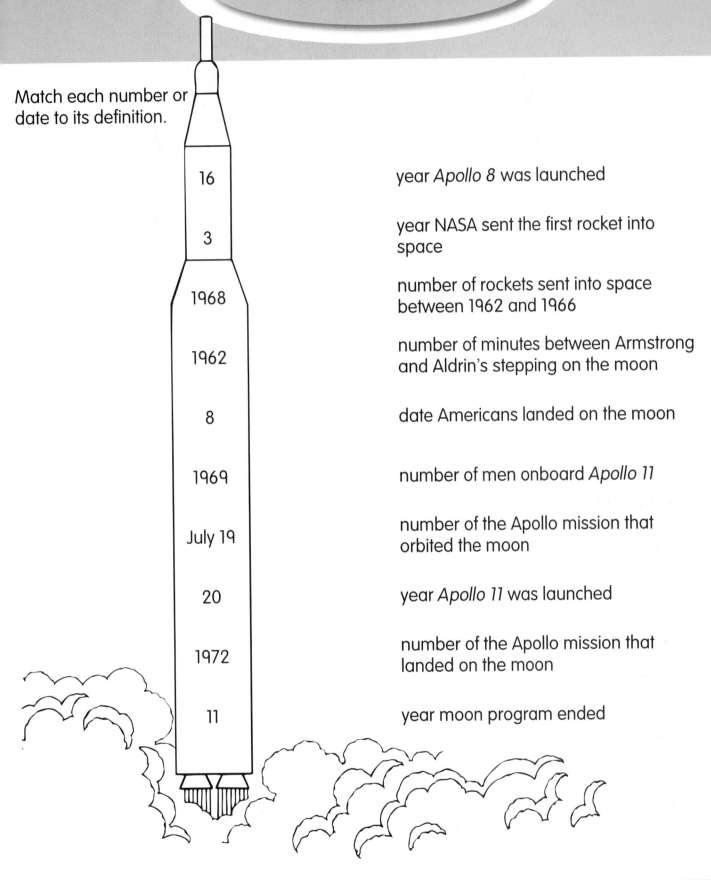

16

3

1968

1962

8

1969

July 19

20

1972

11

year *Apollo 8* was launched

year NASA sent the first rocket into space

number of rockets sent into space between 1962 and 1966

number of minutes between Armstrong and Aldrin's stepping on the moon

date Americans landed on the moon

number of men onboard *Apollo 11*

number of the Apollo mission that orbited the moon

year *Apollo 11* was launched

number of the Apollo mission that landed on the moon

year moon program ended

During the 1960s, the United States and a country called the Soviet Union each wanted to be first to land a person on the moon. The contest was called the "space race."

You and a friend can have your own space race using the game on the next page. Use coins, paper clips, or other small objects for markers.

Flip a coin to see how far to move on each turn. For heads, move 1 space. For tails, move 2 spaces.

Landing on the Moon

START

YOU TEST YOUR EQUIPMENT SUCCESSFULLY. MOVE AHEAD 2 SPACES.

BAD WEATHER PROHIBITS TAKE OFF. MOVE BACK 3 SPACES.

ANOTHER COUNTRY SENDS A ROCKET INTO SPACE. LOSE A TURN.

YOU ORBIT THE EARTH. MOVE AHEAD 1 SPACE.

YOU SUCCESSFULLY LIFT OFF INTO SPACE. MOVE AHEAD 1 SPACE.

YOUR SPACESHIP IS ALMOST AT THE MOON. TAKE ANOTHER TURN.

THERE'S A POWER FAILURE ON THE SPACESHIP! LOSE A TURN.

Kachina Dolls

The Hopi people of the western United States believe that spirits are found in all parts of life. These spirits are called "the cloud people," or kachinas. Kachinas can represent the Earth, the sky, the sun, the animals, and many other natural elements. The Hopi ask the kachinas to help them with rich harvests, good health, and a long life. Between December and July, the Hopi hold important ceremonies to honor the spirit world.

For centuries, Hopi artists have carved kachina dolls to represent these spirits. It is a great honor to have one of these dolls or receive one as a gift.

Kachina dolls are usually made from the root of the cottonwood tree. The artist seasons the wood with a special clay. Then he or she decorates the figure with paints made from natural materials. Other items from nature, such as plants or feathers, are also added. The dolls carry tools, weapons, and other items. The doll is usually performing an action.

The Hopi use kachina dolls to represent the spirits during religious rituals. The dolls were never meant to be toys. Today, kachina dolls are valued as works of art. Many people collect these figures. Many more visit museums to see these dolls and learn about their place in Native American culture.

U.S. Facts & Fun • EMC 6306 • ©2005 by Evan-Moor Corp.

Show What You Know!

Solve this kachina crossword puzzle.

Across

2. Kachinas are often decorated with ___ ___ ___ ___ ___ ___.

4. The Hopi believe that ___ ___ ___ ___ ___ ___ ___ are part of everyday life.

6. Kachinas are carved from the root of

the ___ ___ ___ ___ ___ ___ ___ ___ ___ tree.

7. Kachinas are often shown holding ___ ___ ___ ___ ___ ___ ___.

8. Today, you can see kachina dolls in ___ ___ ___ ___ ___ ___ ___.

Down

1. Kachinas are also called the "___ ___ ___ ___ ___ people."

3. Artists decorate kachinas with items from ___ ___ ___ ___ ___ ___.

5. The Hopi use kachina dolls during religious ___ ___ ___ ___ ___ ___ ___.

Colorful Kachinas

The Hopi painted their kachinas with colors made from natural materials. Earth tones as well as rainbow hues were used.

Color this kachina to make it appear as authentic as possible.

Your Choice

We've given you two possible answers for each math problem below. Choose the correct answer. Then write the letter that matches that answer in the box. The letters will spell the name of the Native American tribe that was the ancestor of the Hopi people.

73 x 3 = 209 = Y
73 x 3 = 219 = A

97 – 69 = 28 = N
97 – 69 = 38 = O

85 + 236 = 312 = C
85 + 236 = 321 = A

58 x 15 = 870 = S
58 x 15 = 970 = E

239 + 456 = 595 = I
239 + 456 = 695 = A

89 x 12 = 1,068 = Z
89 x 12 = 968 = R

943 – 856 = 107 = O
943 – 856 = 87 = I

The Jamestown Colony

About 400 years ago, 144 men and boys sailed from England to a strange new land called North America. These travelers hoped to find gold and silver in the new land.

When the ships reached North America, they sailed across Chesapeake Bay. The settlers found a large river and named it the James River, after King James I of England. They decided to build their new home on the river. They named the settlement Jamestown.

Life was difficult in Jamestown. The water in the river was salty and muddy. Many people became sick from drinking the bad water. Others fell ill because they could not find enough good food. The men did not know how to hunt or fish. They were not used to working hard. More than half of the colonists died the first year.

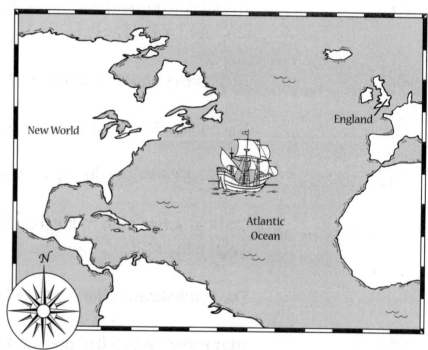

One of the leaders was Captain John Smith. He became friendly with Native Americans in the area. These natives helped the colonists survive until food and supplies arrived from England. Later, the settlers began growing tobacco and selling it to people in England. After several years, Jamestown was a thriving community.

The English colonists never did find gold or silver in Jamestown. But they did establish the first permanent English settlement in the land that would one day become the United States.

U.S. Facts & Fun • EMC 6306 • ©2005 by Evan-Moor Corp.

Show What You Know!

Write whether each statement is *true* or *false*.

1 _____ The first European settlers in America arrived after 1700.

2 _____ The settlers came to America for farmland.

3 _____ The settlers named the James River and Jamestown after King James I of England.

4 _____ The settlers came to America by ship.

5 _____ The James River was a good source of fresh water.

6 _____ Many settlers died during the first year.

7 _____ Captain John Smith made friends with Native Americans who helped the settlers.

8 _____ The Jamestown settlers grew tobacco and sold it to England.

9 _____ Jamestown was full of gold and silver.

10 _____ Jamestown was the first permanent English settlement in America.

Jamestown JUMBLE

Unscramble each word below. The numbers will tell you the paragraph where the word appears in the story. Then unscramble the circled letters to find out the name of John Smith's Native American friend.

RACEMIA (1) __ __ __ __ __ __ (○)

VEATIN (4) __ (○) __ __ __ __

LGDO (1) __ (○) __ __

KPSAEHEEAC (2) __ __ __ __ __ (○) __ __ __ __

CTAOCBO (4) __ __ __ __ __ (○) __

STLSEERT (2) __ __ (○) __ __ __ __ __

OONLITSCS (3) (○) __ __ (○) __ __ __ __ __

GHITIVNR (4) __ (○) __ __ __ __ __ __

PLUSPIES (4) __ __ __ __ __ __ (○) __

Circled letters: __ __ __ __ __ __ __ __ __ __ __ __

Answer: __ __ __ __ __ __ __ __

U.S. Facts & Fun • EMC 6306 • ©2005 by Evan-Moor Corp.

Jamestown Maze

This colonist has gotten lost in the woods! Can you help him find his way back to Jamestown?

ACROSS AMERICA
in a Covered Wagon

If your family were moving to a new home, how would you travel? You might load all your things into a truck and drive across the country. When the pioneers moved into the western United States, they traveled in covered wagons, not cars or trucks. And their journey was a lot different than yours would be today!

A covered wagon was made of wood and iron. It had big wheels that could travel over rough ground. An open space in the back held the family's things. There was room up front for a few people to ride. A canvas cover was stretched over the top to provide shelter from rain, snow, wind, and sun. A covered wagon could carry about 2,000 pounds. It was pulled by horses or oxen.

Pioneers had to pack carefully for their journey. They packed huge sacks of flour, beans, rice, and sugar, plus bacon, hard bread, and dried fruit. Tools and farm equipment were also brought, along with rope, nails, pots, clothes, and other supplies.

Most pioneers traveled along the Oregon Trail. This trail led from Independence, Missouri, to Oregon City, Oregon. It crossed rivers, prairies, deserts, and mountains. The journey was dangerous, so wagons traveled in groups, called wagon trains. A 2,000-mile trip took about four months.

The wagon's work was not done once the pioneers reached their new home! The canvas cover might provide a roof for a log cabin. The wood was used to make new furniture. The wagon that brought the family west became part of their new home.

U.S. Facts & Fun • EMC 6306 • ©2005 by Evan-Moor Corp.

Show What You Know!

Choose the best answer to finish each sentence below.

1 A covered wagon was made of _____ .
   a. wood and iron
   b. plastic
   c. logs

2 The wagon had big wheels because _____ .
   a. people liked to be high above
      the ground
   b. they helped the wagon travel faster
   c. they could travel over rough ground

3 The wagon was filled with _____ .
   a. farm animals
   b. food and tools
   c. refreshments

4 The Oregon Trail led from _____ .
   a. Oregon to Nebraska
   b. Missouri to Oregon
   c. Missouri to California

5 The journey west took about _____ .
   a. one year
   b. six months
   c. four months

6 Wagon trains provided _____ .
   a. entertainment
   b. traffic jams
   c. safety

7 Once in their new home, the
   pioneers often _____ .
   a. used parts of the wagon to
      build a house
   b. used the wagon to ride to town
   c. sold the wagon to another family

Map ADVENTURES

Look at the map on the next page to answer the questions.

1 On what river is the town of Independence, Missouri, located?

_____

2 Is Fort Kearny east or west of the Continental Divide?

_____

3 Heading west, will the travelers reach Fort Laramie or Fort Bridger first?

_____

4 What is the name of the basin west of the Rocky Mountains?

_____

5 What river flows by Fort Hall?

_____

6 In which direction does the trail go after Fort Boise?

_____

7 What is the last mountain range before Oregon City?

_____

8 What Oregon river flows into the Pacific Ocean?

_____

The Oregon Trail

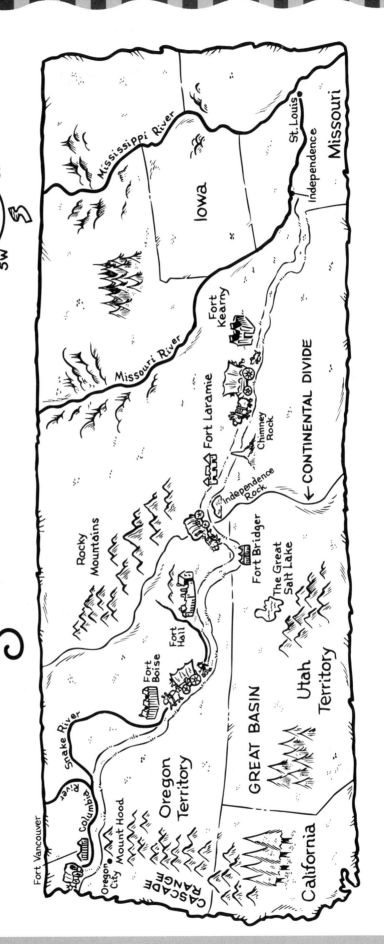

THE MIGHTY MISSISSIPPI

If you stand on the shore of Lake Itasca in Minnesota, you'll see a tiny stream flowing out of the lake. This small beginning leads to great things. This stream is the start of the Mississippi River.

The Mississippi River is the second-longest river in the United States. It flows for 2,340 miles from northern Minnesota to the Gulf of Mexico. The river gets its name from a Native American word that means "big river." Other natives called it "the father of waters."

In some places, the Mississippi is filled with rough rapids. In other places, it is wide and deep. When it reaches the Gulf of Mexico, the river flows through a wide delta, or low-lying plain. Along its path, many other rivers, or tributaries, flow into the Mississippi.

Most of the time, the Mississippi River is a wonderful resource. The land near the river is excellent for farming. Cities and towns have grown up along the banks. Thousands of plants and animals live in and along the river. The Mississippi is also a major transportation route and source of drinking water.

The Mississippi, however, has also caused a lot of trouble. Over the years, floods have devastated towns along the river. Thousands of people lost their homes when the Mississippi overflowed its banks and covered farmland, streets, and houses. The Mississippi displays its might in both positive and negative ways.

U.S. Facts & Fun • EMC 6306 • ©2005 by Evan-Moor Corp.

Draw a line to match each word on the right with the correct definition on the left.

a certain road or way   delta

to flood over the edges   rapids

land along the sides of a river   devastate

fast, rough water   overflow

rivers that flow into a larger river   route

to damage badly   tributaries

flat plain where a river deposits mud   resource

something valuable or useful   banks

Mississippi riverboats were powered by steam that turned a large paddle wheel at the back of the boat. Unscramble the letters to find out a nickname for this type of boat.

NEWHTSEERELR

__ t __ __ __ w __ __ e __ __ __

SCRAMBLED STATES

The Mississippi flows by or through 10 states. Can you unscramble the name of each of these states below? Use the map on the next page to help you.

OMNTINEAS __ __ __ __ __ __ __ __ __

WIAO __ __ __ __

SLOILINI __ __ __ __ __ __ __ __

UNALSIOIA __ __ __ __ __ __ __ __ __

NISCWNOSI __ __ __ __ __ __ __ __ __

TNEUKCYK __ __ __ __ __ __ __ __

ASKSRANA __ __ __ __ __ __ __ __

ENTNSEESE __ __ __ __ __ __ __ __ __

IPSMSISIPSI __ __ __ __ __ __ __ __ __ __ __

ORSISIMU __ __ __ __ __ __ __ __

U.S. Facts & Fun • EMC 6306 • ©2005 by Evan-Moor Corp.

A TRIP DOWN THE MISSISSIPPI

Come journey down the 2,340-mile length of the Mississippi from its small beginnings. You'll see many interesting sites. Number these sights in the order you would see them.

☐ Gateway Arch towering above the riverbanks at St. Louis

☐ A Mardi Gras parade in this city near the Mississippi Delta

☐ A small stream leaving Lake Itasca

☐ Fishing boats heading out into the waters of the Gulf of Mexico

☐ A Civil War memorial commemorating the Battle of Vicksburg

☐ The Twin Cities, one on each side of the river

☐ The largest city in Tennessee

MINNESOTA
Lake Itasca
St. Paul
Minneapolis
WISCONSIN
IOWA
ILLINOIS
KENTUCKY
St. Louis
MISSOURI
TENNESSEE
ARKANSAS
Memphis
MISSISSIPPI
LOUISIANA
Vicksburg
New Orleans
Mississippi Delta
Gulf of Mexico

"I Will Fight No More Forever" — Chief Joseph

Throughout our history, Native American tribes have suffered greatly at the hands of the U.S. government. In many cases, even those who did not want to fight became victims. The story of the Nez Perce and their leader Chief Joseph is a sad example.

Joseph was born around 1840 in the Wallowa Valley of eastern Oregon. His father was the chief of the tribe. When Joseph was young, his father agreed to help white settlers. In return, the U.S. government promised it would never take the Nez Perce's land.

Joseph became chief in 1871. By then, gold had been discovered in the Wallowa Valley. Before long, the government broke its promise. It told the Nez Perce that they had to move to a reservation* in Idaho.

Chief Joseph did not want to go to the reservation. He did not want to fight the government either. Instead, he led his people toward Canada. The U.S. Army followed him.

The Nez Perce stayed free for 115 days. They traveled across Oregon, Washington, Idaho, and Montana. Finally, the army caught up with them in October 1877. Chief Joseph surrendered. "I will fight no more forever," he said.

The Nez Perce were sent to Oklahoma. Most of the tribe died there. In 1885, Chief Joseph and the remainder of the tribe were forced to march to a reservation in Washington. Chief Joseph died there in 1904. To this day, his courage is remembered and admired.

*reservation: land set aside by the government for a particular reason

U.S. Facts & Fun • EMC 6306 • ©2005 by Evan-Moor Corp.

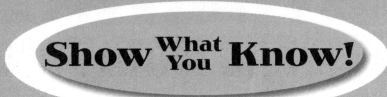

Number these events in the order in which they happened.

☐ The U.S. government demanded that the Nez Perce move to Idaho.

☐ Chief Joseph died.

☐ Joseph became chief.

☐ Chief Joseph surrendered.

☐ The U.S. government promised never to take the Nez Perce's land.

☐ Chief Joseph was born.

☐ Chief Joseph tried to lead his people to Canada.

☐ The Nez Perce were sent to Oklahoma.

☐ Chief Joseph and his tribe were sent to Washington.

On the Map

The map on the next page shows the journey of Chief Joseph and the Nez Perce. Use it to answer the questions.

1 How many battles did the Nez Perce fight along their journey?

_____

2 How long did it take to travel from White Bird Canyon to Fort Fizzle?

_____

3 In which direction did the Nez Perce travel to get from Fort Missoula to Big Hole?

_____

4 In which two directions did the U.S. Army travel when they left Fort Keogh?

_____

5 In which direction would you travel to get from Fort Ellis to Fort Shaw?

_____

6 What were the names of the two mountain ranges between Lolo Pass and Canyon Creek?

_____

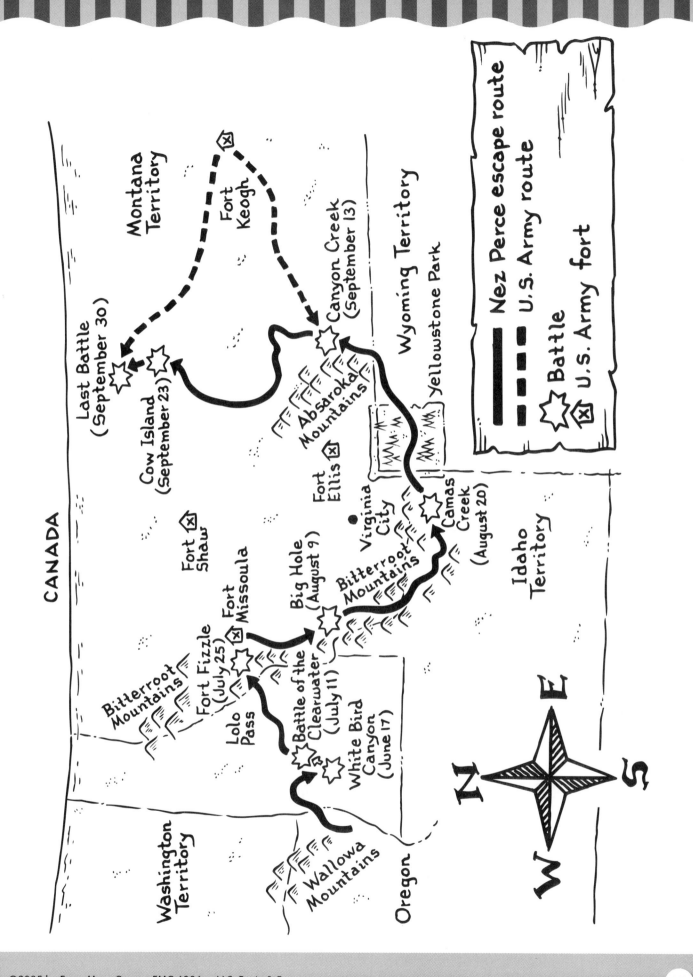

CANADA

Montana Territory

Fort Keogh

Last Battle
(September 30)

Cow Island
(September 23)

Canyon Creek
(September 13)

Wyoming Territory

Yellowstone Park

Absaroka Mountains

Fort Ellis

Virginia City

Camas Creek
(August 20)

Idaho Territory

Fort Shaw

Bitterroot Mountains

Fort Missoula

Big Hole
(August 9)

Bitterroot Mountains

Fort Fizzle
(July 25)

Lolo Pass

Battle of the Clearwater
(July 11)

White Bird Canyon
(June 17)

Washington Territory

Wallowa Mountains

Oregon

Nez Perce escape route
U.S. Army route
Battle
U.S. Army fort

N E W S

BASEBALL—
America's Game

Americans have been enjoying baseball for more than 150 years. The first baseball game was played in Hoboken, New Jersey, in 1846. Although the game was called baseball, it was very different from the game we play today. The pitcher threw underhand. It took nine balls, not four, to walk a batter. The distance between the pitcher's mound and home plate was much shorter, too.

Each era has had its own baseball heroes. During the 1920s and 1930s, Babe Ruth was the king of the game. Ruth was a famous home-run hitter for the New York Yankees. During some years, he hit more home runs than entire teams did!

At first, all major-league players were white. Then Jackie Robinson became the first black major-leaguer in 1947. By the 1970s, many of the game's greatest players were black Americans, including Roberto Clemente, Willie Mays, and Hank Aaron.

Baseball isn't just for major-league players. It is also a game many children enjoy. Thousands of boys and girls take part in Little League games and dream of playing in the Little League World Series. Thousands more play just for fun in backyards, vacant lots, and fields. Other children—and grown-ups, too—enjoy keeping track of the game's action on a scorecard.

Every season brings new excitement and new records. In baseball, the crack of the bat always means something exciting is about to happen!

U.S. Facts & Fun • EMC 6306 • ©2005 by Evan-Moor Corp.

Write whether each statement is *true* or *false*.

1 _____ The first baseball game was played about 75 years ago.

2 _____ The first baseball game was played in New Jersey.

3 _____ The rules of baseball have always stayed the same.

4 _____ Babe Ruth was a popular home-run hitter for the New York Yankees.

5 _____ Many black Americans played in the Major Leagues before 1947.

6 _____ Jackie Robinson was the first black American to play in the Major Leagues.

7 _____ Only grown-ups can enjoy baseball.

8 _____ The Little League has its own World Series.

9 _____ Many children play baseball in their own neighborhoods.

10 _____ A scorecard is used to keep track of the action in a game.

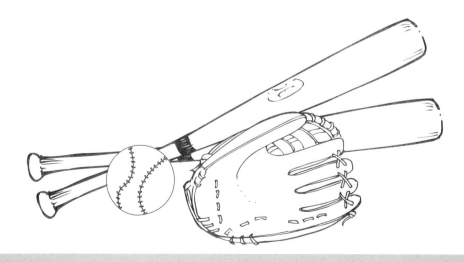

BASEBALL
Kriss-Kross

Today, there are 30 major-league teams. Can you fit all the team names into the puzzle grid on the next page? You will have to use logic!

4 letters
Cubs
Mets
Reds

5 letters
Expos
Twins

6 letters
Angels
Astros
Braves
Giants
Padres
Red Sox
Royals
Tigers

7 letters
Brewers
Dodgers
Indians
Marlins
Orioles
Pirates
Rangers
Rockies
Yankees

8 letters
Blue Jays
Mariners
Phillies
White Sox

9 letters
Athletics
Cardinals
Devil Rays

12 letters
Diamondbacks

HINT: Start with the one 12-letter word.

U.S. Facts & Fun • EMC 6306 • ©2005 by Evan-Moor Corp.

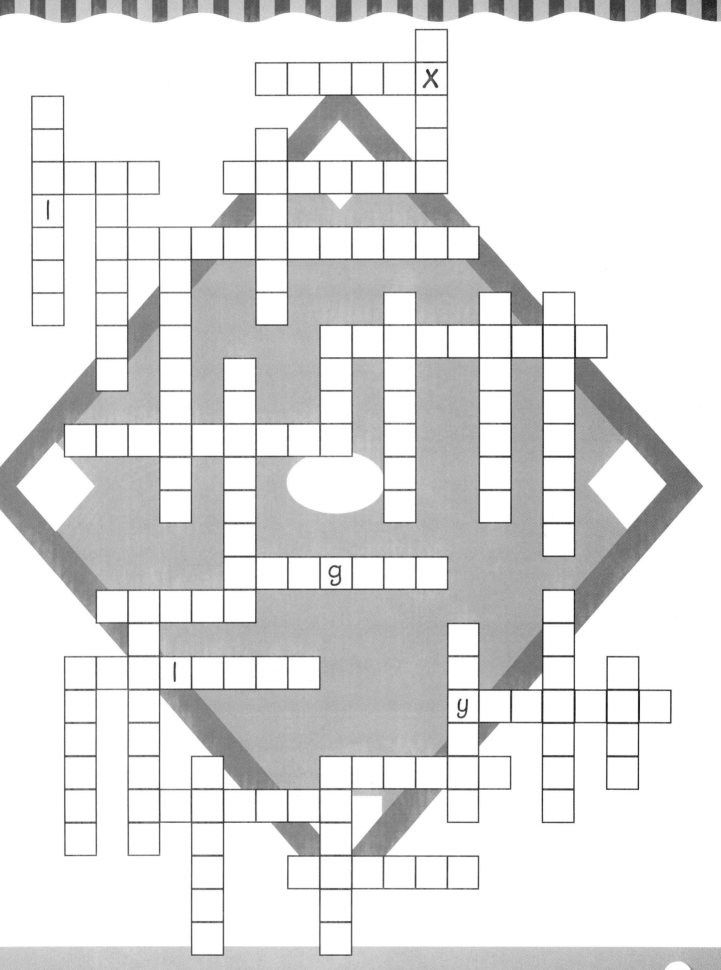

The GREAT Lakes

There are many lakes in the United States, but only five are officially "Great." The Great Lakes border eight states and two Canadian provinces. Together, these lakes contain 18 percent of all the fresh water in the world. The only place that has more fresh water is the polar ice cap!

Lake Superior is the largest of the Great Lakes. It is also the largest freshwater lake in the world. Lake Huron is the second-largest Great Lake. Huron contains a bay that is so big, it is sometimes called "the sixth Great Lake." One of Lake Michigan's most interesting features is actually outside the lake. This lake is surrounded by huge sand dunes.

Lake Erie was part of an important early transportation system. During the early 1800s, the Erie Canal was built to link this lake with the Hudson River in Albany, New York. Lake Ontario is the smallest of the Great Lakes. It is the farthest east and forms part of the border between the state of New York and Canada.

The Great Lakes were formed thousands of years ago by gigantic, heavy sheets of ice, called glaciers. As the glaciers moved, they scraped huge holes in the land. When the climate warmed up, the glaciers melted and filled the holes with water. Today, the Great Lakes provide a source of transportation, food, drinking water, and recreation for the residents of two nations.

Ⓐ Lake Superior
Ⓑ Lake Michigan
Ⓒ Lake Huron
Ⓓ Lake Erie
Ⓔ Lake Ontario

U.S. Facts & Fun • EMC 6306 • ©2005 by Evan-Moor Corp.

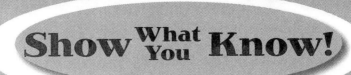

> Write the names of the Great Lakes from largest to smallest below.

1 Lake ☐ __ ▨ __ __ __ __

2 Lake ☐ __ __ __ __

3 Lake ☐ __ __ __ __ __ ▨ __

4 Lake ▨ ☐ __ __

5 Lake __ __ ▨ ☐ __ __ __

> Next, rearrange the boxed letters to spell the name of an area of wet, low-lying land around a lake.

Boxed letters: ☐ ☐ ☐ ☐ ☐

Answer: __ __ __ __ __

> Now, rearrange the shaded letters to spell the name of the type of moss that grows in the area you spelled out above.

Shaded letters: __ __ __ __

Answer: __ __ __ __

WORD SQUARES

Each lake below contains an 8-letter word from the story. Find each word by reading either clockwise or counterclockwise around the lake.

H I G
C   A
I M N

_____

O I R
R   E
S U P

_____

C N I
E   V
P R O

_____

A N A
C   D
N A I

_____

R S G
E   L
I C A

_____

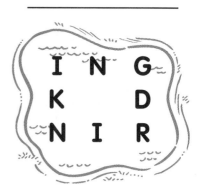

I N G
K   D
N I R

_____

U.S. Facts & Fun • EMC 6306 • ©2005 by Evan-Moor Corp.

LAKE LOCATIONS
CROSSWORD

In the puzzle below, write the names of the eight states and two Canadian provinces that border the Great Lakes. Each clue is the abbreviation for that state or province. You may need to use an atlas to help you.

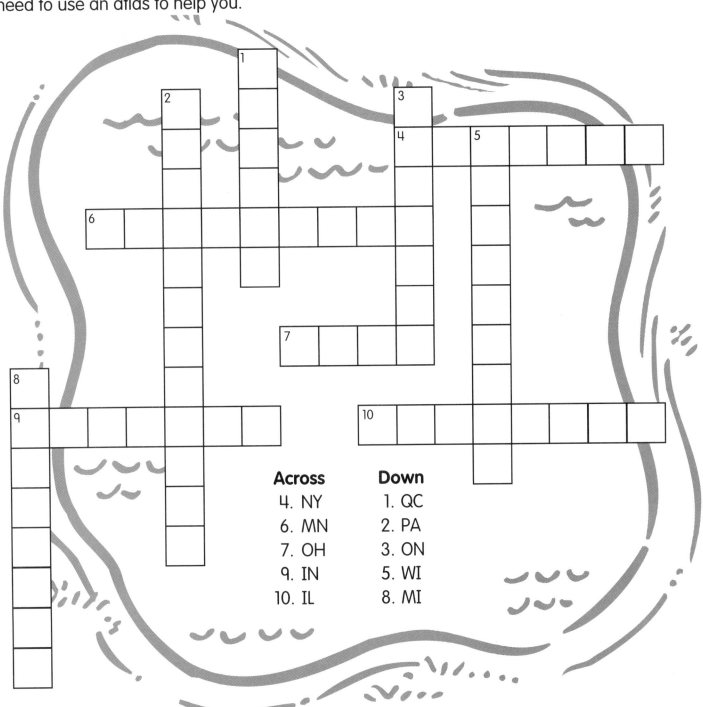

Across
4. NY
6. MN
7. OH
9. IN
10. IL

Down
1. QC
2. PA
3. ON
5. WI
8. MI

THE PONY EXPRESS

In 1860, sending mail was not as easy as it is today. In those days, many letters were sent by ship. Other mail was given to travelers passing through town on wagon trains. It could take months before a letter arrived —if it arrived at all.

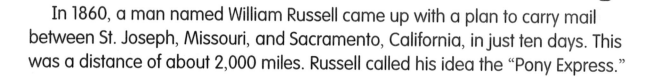

In 1860, a man named William Russell came up with a plan to carry mail between St. Joseph, Missouri, and Sacramento, California, in just ten days. This was a distance of about 2,000 miles. Russell called his idea the "Pony Express."

The Pony Express began on April 3, 1860. It used young men riding fast horses to deliver the mail. Along the way, stations provided fresh horses, food, water, and a place to sleep. Riders were paid about $25 a week to get the mail through, no matter what. The Pony Express advertised for "expert riders willing to risk death daily." Death could come from Indian attacks, bad weather, or natural disasters.

The Pony Express was a huge success. However, the invention of the telegraph doomed the Pony Express. On October 24, 1861, a telegraph message was sent from San Francisco to Washington, D.C. News could now be sent across miles in just a few minutes. Two days later, on October 26, the Pony Express made its last run.

The Pony Express lasted for only 18 months, but it captured the hearts of people all over the world. Stories of the Pony Express riders and their horses are full of adventure and danger. They are an important and exciting part of American history.

Match each number or date to its definition.

1860

25

April 3, 1860

2,000

October 24, 1861

October 26, 1861

18

10

the first telegraph message was sent across the country

number of months the Pony Express lasted

dollars a week earned by riders

the Pony Express ended

William Russell came up with the idea for the Pony Express

number of days it took mail to travel from Missouri to California

the Pony Express began

number of miles between Missouri and California

A PAIR OF HORSES

Only two of these Pony Express horses are exactly alike. Can you find them?

U.S. Facts & Fun • EMC 6306 • ©2005 by Evan-Moor Corp.

MAIL MAZE

Can you help this Pony Express rider get to his next stop? Mark his path through the maze.

Separated States —
Alaska and Hawaii

Forty-eight of the fifty U.S. states have borders that touch other states. Alaska and Hawaii are different. These states are separated from the rest of the nation.

Alaska is the largest and wildest place in the United States. It is twice as big as the state of Texas. Its coastline is longer than all the coasts in the mainland states put together. Alaska is also home to North America's highest mountain. This mountain has two names, Mount McKinley or Denali. Alaska also has the world's longest chain of active volcanoes and more glaciers than the rest of the planet. Despite its huge size, Alaska has a small population. Most of the state's people live along the southern coast.

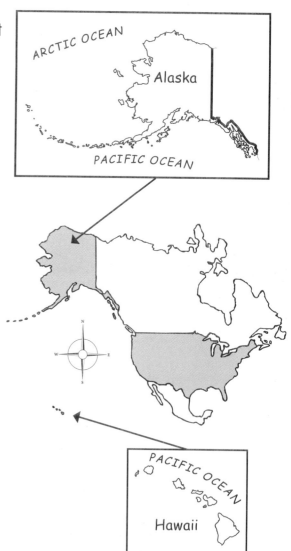

The United States bought Alaska from Russia in 1867. It became the 49th state in 1959. That same year, Hawaii became the 50th U.S. state. Like Alaska, Hawaii is very different from the rest of the United States. This state is actually a chain of islands located in the middle of the Pacific Ocean. Hawaii has a warm, wet climate. It is a land of ocean shores and waving palm trees.

Hawaii was originally settled by Polynesians from other Pacific Islands. Later, many people came from Japan and China to harvest pineapples and sugar. Hawaii is a beautiful place where people of many different races live together. Like Alaska, it is a unique and special part of the United States.

U.S. Facts & Fun • EMC 6306 • ©2005 by Evan-Moor Corp.

Show What You Know!

Read each statement below. Fill in the blanks by writing *Hawaii* or *Alaska* to complete each statement.

1. _____ is in the middle of the Pacific Ocean.

2. The U.S. bought _____ from Russia in 1867.

3. _____ is the largest state in the nation.

4. _____ is a chain of islands.

5. _____ has more glaciers than the rest of the world.

6. _____ has a warm, wet climate.

7. Many people came to _____ from China and Japan.

8. North America's largest mountain is located in _____ .

9. _____ has a small population.

10. _____ became the 50th state in 1959.

A Separated State – Alaska

Use the map of Alaska to answer these questions:

1. Which country borders Alaska?

   _____

2. What is the name of the chain of islands that stretch out into the Pacific Ocean?

   _____

3. What is the capital of Alaska?

   _____

4. To visit Kuskokwim River, in what direction would you travel from Anchorage?

   _____

5. How many mountain ranges are shown on this map?

   _____

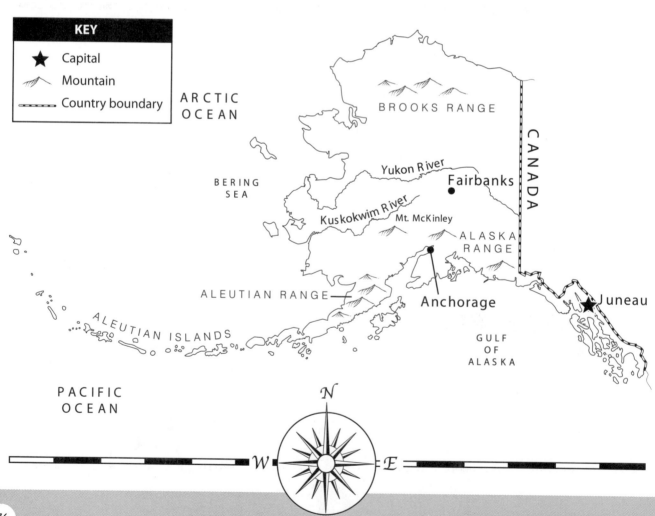

KEY

★ Capital

Mountain

Country boundary

ARCTIC OCEAN

BROOKS RANGE

CANADA

Yukon River

Fairbanks

BERING SEA

Kuskokwim River

Mt. McKinley

ALASKA RANGE

ALEUTIAN RANGE

Anchorage

Juneau

ALEUTIAN ISLANDS

GULF OF ALASKA

PACIFIC OCEAN

N

W   E

S

A Separated State – Hawaii

Use the map of Hawaii to answer these questions:

1. How many main islands make up the state of Hawaii? _____

2. What is the capital of Hawaii and on what island is it located? _____
   _____

3. Which island is the largest? _____

4. For what geological feature is Hawaii known? _____

5. In which direction would you travel to go from Kauai
   to Hawaii? _____

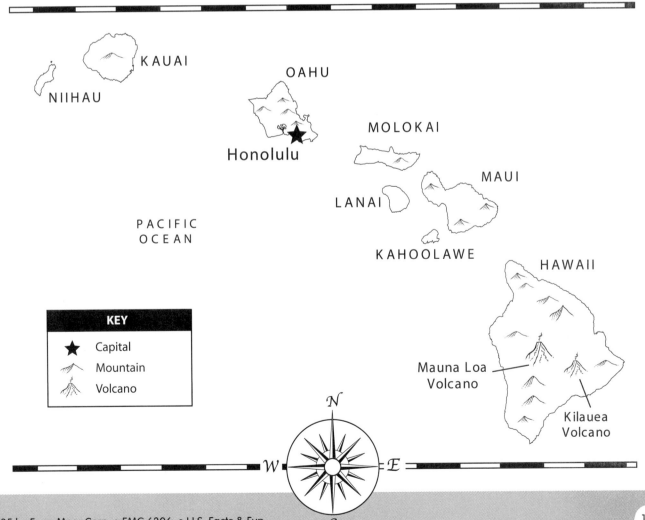

KAUAI

NIIHAU

OAHU

Honolulu

MOLOKAI

MAUI

LANAI

PACIFIC
OCEAN

KAHOOLAWE

HAWAII

Mauna Loa
Volcano

Kilauea
Volcano

KEY
★ Capital
Mountain
Volcano

N
W   E
S

Answer Key

Page 3

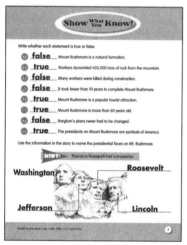

Show What You Know!

Write whether each statement is true or false.

1. **false** Mount Rushmore is a natural formation.
2. **true** Workers dynamited 450,000 tons of rock from the mountain.
3. **false** Many workers were killed during construction.
4. **false** It took fewer than 10 years to complete Mount Rushmore.
5. **true** Mount Rushmore is a popular tourist attraction.
6. **true** Mount Rushmore is more than 60 years old.
7. **false** Borglum's plans never had to be changed.
8. **true** The presidents on Mount Rushmore are symbols of America.

Use the information in the story to name the presidential faces on Mt. Rushmore.

HINT: Theodore Roosevelt had a mustache.

Washington **Roosevelt**

Jefferson **Lincoln**

Page 4

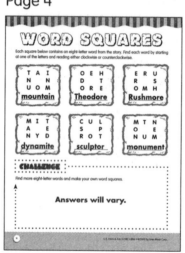

WORD SQUARES

Each square below contains an eight-letter word from the story. Find each word by starting at one of the letters and reading either clockwise or counterclockwise.

mountain **Theodore** **Rushmore**

dynamite **sculptor** **monument**

CHALLENGE

Find more eight-letter words and make your own word squares.

Answers will vary.

Page 5

The A-Maze-ing MOUNTAIN These tourists want to explore Mount Rushmore. Can you help them find their way through the mountain maze?

Page 7

Show What You Know!

Number these events in the order in which they happened.

- **5** Crockett became a U.S. Congressman.
- **3** Crockett got a job driving cattle.
- **2** Crockett ran away from home after a fight.
- **7** Crockett was killed defending the Alamo.
- **8** Movies were made about Crockett's life.
- **4** Crockett was elected to the Tennessee legislature.
- **1** Crockett listened to stories at his father's tavern.
- **6** Crockett volunteered for the Texas army.

CHALLENGE

Write another detail about Davy Crockett's life. What two numbers would it come between in the above sequence?

Answers will vary.

It would come between number _____ and number _____.

Page 8

HIDDEN PICTURES

When he lived in the wilderness, Davy Crockett had to hunt to survive. Can you find six hidden animals in the forest below? Color them.

Page 9

DAVY CROCKETT SCRAMBLE Unscramble the words below and write them on the lines. Then unscramble the shaded letters to find out what item of clothing Crockett was famous for wearing.

HINT: The number after each scrambled word tells you the paragraph where the word can be found.

NESESETNE (1) **TENNESSEE**

LTACTE (2) **CATTLE**

ECNEEDNPENID (4) **INDEPENDENCE**

REOFITNR (1) **FRONTIER**

KLSSLI (2) **SKILLS**

LOAMAN (4) **ALAMO**

XCEMOI (4) **MEXICO**

Shaded letters: **NSCNPOKAOIC**

Item of Clothing **COONSKIN CAP**

Page 11

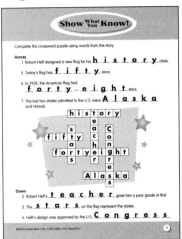

Show What You Know!

Complete the crossword puzzle using words from the story.

Across
1. Robert Heft designed a new flag for his **h i s t o r y** class.
5. Today's flag has **f i f t y** stars.
6. In 1958, the American flag had **forty-eight** stars.
7. The last two states admitted to the U.S. were **A l a s k a** and Hawaii.

Down
2. Robert Heft's **t e a c h e r** gave him a poor grade at first.
3. The **s t a r s** on the flag represent the states.
4. Heft's design was approved by the U.S. **C o n g r e s s**

Page 12

STARRY CODE

Use the numbered code below to figure out the name of a famous song about the U.S. flag.

12 × 12 = **144** = A   13 × 13 = **169** = T   16 × 14 = **224** = S
78 ÷ 54 = **132** = D   92 − 27 = **65** = N   219 − 138 = **81** = P
51 − 36 = **15** = E   109 − 64 = **45** = O   54 × 3 = **162** = V
19 × 3 = **57** = F   25 + 216 = **241** = P
62 + 89 = **151** = H   269 + 47 = **316** = R

T H E   S T A R S   A N D
81 151 15   224 81 144 316 224   144 65 132

S T R I P E S   F O R E V E R
224 81 316 169 241 15 224   57 45 316 162 15 316

Page 13

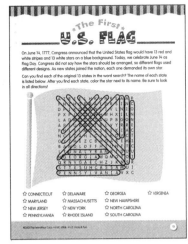

The First U.S. FLAG

On June 14, 1777, Congress announced that the United States flag would have 13 red and white stripes and 13 white stars on a blue background. Today, we celebrate June 14 as Flag Day. Congress did not say how the stars should be arranged, so different flags used different designs. As new states joined the nation, each one demanded its own star.

Can you find each of the original 13 states in the word search? The name of each state is listed below. After you find each state, color the star next to its name. Be sure to look in all directions!

☆ CONNECTICUT   ☆ DELAWARE   ☆ GEORGIA   ☆ VIRGINIA
☆ MARYLAND   ☆ MASSACHUSETTS ☆ NEW HAMPSHIRE
☆ NEW JERSEY   ☆ NEW YORK   ☆ NORTH CAROLINA
☆ PENNSYLVANIA   ☆ RHODE ISLAND ☆ SOUTH CAROLINA

Page 15

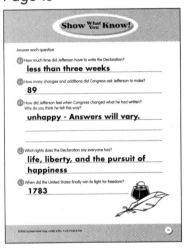

Show What You Know!

Answer each question.

1. How much time did Jefferson have to write the Declaration?
less than three weeks

2. How many changes and additions did Congress ask Jefferson to make?
89

3. How did Jefferson feel when Congress changed what he had written? Why do you think he felt this way?
unhappy - Answers will vary.

4. What rights does the Declaration say everyone has?
life, liberty, and the pursuit of happiness

5. When did the United States finally win its fight for freedom?
1783

Page 16

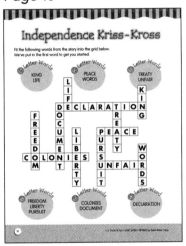

Independence Kriss-Kross

Fit the following words from the story into the grid below. We've put in the first word to get you started.

4 Letter Words
KING
LIFE

4 Letter Words
PEACE
WORDS

6 Letter Words
TREATY
UNFAIR

7 Letter Words
FREEDOM
LIBERTY
PURSUIT

8 Letter Words
COLONIES
DOCUMENT

11 Letter Word
DECLARATION

Page 17

Hidden Quills

Thomas Jefferson wrote the Declaration of Independence with a quill pen. A quill pen is made from a bird's feather, or quill. The tip is dipped into ink in order to write.

Find and color seven quill pens hidden in the picture below.

Page 19

Show What You Know!

Fill in the blanks with words from the story to complete each sentence below. Then put the numbered letters in order to spell the name of another food George Washington Carver found many uses for.

1. Cotton was the most popular crop in the **s o u t h e r n** United States.
2. Carver was a **t e a c h e r** at Tuskegee Institute.
3. The Tuskegee Institute was in **A l a b a m a**.
4. Originally, peanuts were only used to **f e e d** animals.
5. Carver found more than 300 **w a y s** to use peanuts.
6. Carver once made a whole meal out of **p e a n u t s**.
7. Peanuts soon became an important **c r o p**.

s w e e t   p o t a t o
1 2 3 4 5   6 7 8 9 10 11

Page 20

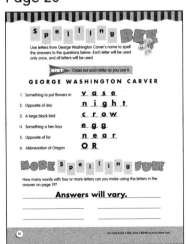

Spelling BEE

Use letters from George Washington Carver's name to spell the answers to the questions below. Each letter will be used only once, and all letters will be used.

HINT: Cross out each letter as you use it.

GEORGE WASHINGTON CARVER

1. Something to put flowers in   **v a s e**
2. Opposite of day   **n i g h t**
3. A large black bird   **c r o w**
4. Something a hen lays   **e g g**
5. Opposite of far   **n e a r**
6. Abbreviation of Oregon   **O R**

MORE Spelling FUN!

How many words with four or more letters can you make using the letters in the answer on page 19?

Answers will vary.

Page 21

PEANUT MATCH-UP

Can you find the two jars of peanut butter that are the same? Circle them.

Page 23

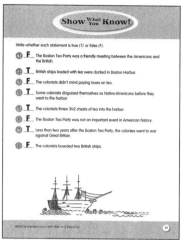

Show What You Know!

Write whether each statement is true (T) or false (F).

1. **F** The Boston Tea Party was a friendly meeting between the Americans and the British.
2. **T** British ships loaded with tea were docked in Boston Harbor.
3. **F** The colonists didn't mind paying taxes on tea.
4. **T** Some colonists disguised themselves as Native-Americans before they went to the harbor.
5. **T** The colonists threw 342 chests of tea into the harbor.
6. **F** The Boston Tea Party was not an important event in American history.
7. **T** Less than two years after the Boston Tea Party, the colonies went to war against Great Britain.
8. **F** The colonists boarded two British ships.

Page 24

Tea Party Maze

Help this colonist find his way back to shore. Find the correct path through the maze.

Page 25

A Patriotic Dot-to-Dot

Connect the dots to see a portrait of an American patriot who lived in Boston at the time of the Boston Tea Party. This man later became the second president of the United States. Unscramble the letters to find his name.

OJNH MADAS

Who is it? **JOHN ADAMS**

Page 27

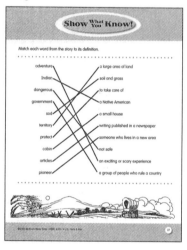

Show What You Know!

Match each word from the story to its definition.

- adventure — an exciting or scary experience
- Indian — a Native American
- dangerous — not safe
- government — a group of people who rule a country
- sod — soil and grass
- territory — a large area of land
- protect — to take care of
- cabin — a small house
- articles — writing published in a newspaper
- pioneer — someone who lives in a new area

Page 29

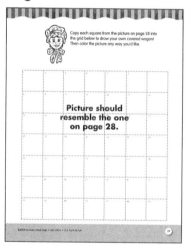

Copy each square from the picture on page 28 into the grid below to draw your own covered wagon! Then color the picture any way you'd like.

Picture should resemble the one on page 28.

Page 31

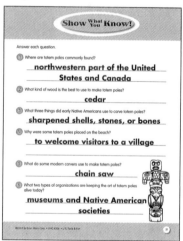

Show What You Know!

Answer each question.

1. Where are totem poles commonly found?
   northwestern part of the United States and Canada
2. What kind of wood is the best to use to make totem poles?
   cedar
3. What three things did early Native Americans use to carve totem poles?
   sharpened shells, stones, or bones
4. Why were some totem poles placed on the beach?
   to welcome visitors to a village
5. What do some modern carvers use to make totem poles?
   chain saw
6. What two types of organizations are keeping the art of totem poles alive today?
   museums and Native American societies

Page 32

Secret Message

Follow the directions to cross out words in the list below. The leftover words will form a sentence. Write the sentence on the lines.

Clue 1: Cross out all words that begin with the letter B.
Clue 2: Cross out all words that end with the letters ING.
Clue 3: Cross out all words that are colors.
Clue 4: Cross out all words that rhyme with three.
Clue 5: Cross out all 3-letter words.

SEWING BIRD RED EUROPEAN KNEE TO EXPLORERS AT BEAR SEE WERE PURPLE AMAZED BINGO GREEN IS WHEN SING FREE THEY YELLOW FIRST DO BROTHER RING SAW ME TOTEM BIKE OF POLES TREE COMING TWO ORANGE ON HUNDRED BOX WHITE PARKING YEARS BOY PINK AGO STRING

European explorers were amazed when they first saw totem poles two hundred years old.

Page 33

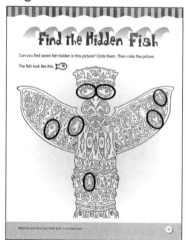

Find the Hidden Fish

Can you find seven fish hidden in this picture? Circle them. Then color the picture.

The fish look like this.

Page 35

Show What You Know!

Write whether each statement is true or false.

1. During Martin's life, black Americans and white Americans were always treated equally. **false**
2. Black children and white children went to different schools. **true**
3. Martin wanted to make the world a better place for his children. **true**
4. Martin gave many speeches during his life. **true**
5. Martin never took his daughter to Funtown. **false**
6. Martin gave his "I have a dream" speech in 1959. **false**
7. Only a few people heard Martin's "I have a dream" speech. **false**
8. Martin helped make things better for black Americans. **true**

OUR HEROES

Page 36

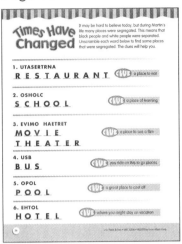

Times Have Changed

It may be hard to believe today, but during Martin's life many places were segregated. This means that black people and white people were separated. Unscramble each word below to find some places that were segregated. The clues will help you.

1. UTASERTRNA
   R E S T A U R A N T **CLUE** a place to eat

2. OSHOLC
   S C H O O L **CLUE** a place of learning

3. EVIMO HAETRET
   M O V I E
   T H E A T E R **CLUE** a place to see a film

4. USB
   B U S **CLUE** you ride on this to go places

5. OPOL
   P O O L **CLUE** a great place to cool off

6. EHTOL
   H O T E L **CLUE** where you might stay on vacation

Page 37

Martin's Maze

These people want to hear Martin's "I have a dream" speech. Help them find their way to the gathering.

Page 39

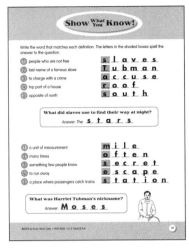

Show What You Know!

Write the word that matches each definition. The letters in the shaded boxes spell the answer to the question.

1. people who are not free — **s l a v e s**
2. last name of a famous slave — **T u b m a n**
3. to charge with a crime — **a c c u s e**
4. top part of a house — **r o o f**
5. opposite of north — **s o u t h**

What did slaves use to find their way at night?
Answer: The **s t a r s**

1. a unit of measurement — **m i l e**
2. many times — **o f t e n**
3. something few people know — **s e c r e t**
4. to run away — **e s c a p e**
5. a place where passengers catch trains — **s t a t i o n**

What was Harriet Tubman's nickname?
Answer: **M o s e s**

Page 40

Help This Runaway

Help this runaway find his way to the next station. Work each math problem and write the answer on the line. Then write the answers in the boxes next to the landmarks on the map on page 41. Draw a trail from the smallest number to the largest number to find the way.

1. 126 − 17 = **109** big rock
2. 96 + 78 = **174** cave
3. 15 x 3 = **45** pine trees
4. 11 x 12 = **132** old shack
5. 96 − 78 = **18** pond
6. 35 + 46 = **81** apple tree

Page 41

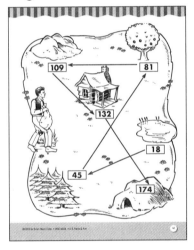

Page 43

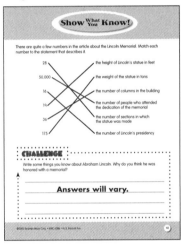

Show What You Know!

There are quite a few numbers in the article about the Lincoln Memorial. Match each number to the statement that describes it.

28 — the height of Lincoln's statue in feet
50,000 — the weight of the statue in tons
16 — the number of columns in the building
19 — the number of people who attended the dedication of the memorial
36 — the number of sections in which the statue was made
175 — the number of Lincoln's presidency

CHALLENGE
Write some things you know about Abraham Lincoln. Why do you think he was honored with a memorial?

Answers will vary.

Page 44

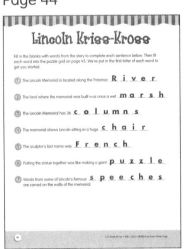

Lincoln Kriss-Kross

Fill in the blanks with words from the story to complete each sentence below. Then fit each word into the puzzle grid on page 45. We've put in the first letter of each word to get you started.

1. The Lincoln Memorial is located along the Potomac **R i v e r**
2. The land where the memorial was built was once a wet **m a r s h**
3. The Lincoln Memorial has 36 **c o l u m n s**
4. The memorial shows Lincoln sitting in a huge **c h a i r**
5. The sculptor's last name was **F r e n c h**
6. Putting the statue together was like making a giant **p u z z l e**
7. Words from some of Lincoln's famous **s p e e c h e s** are carved on the walls of the memorial.

Page 45

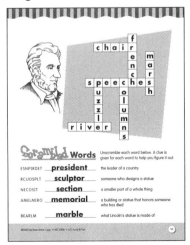

Scrambled Words

Unscramble each word below. A clue is given for each word to help you figure it out.

ESNPIRDET — **president** — the leader of a country
RCUOSPLT — **sculptor** — someone who designs a statue
NECOSIT — **section** — a smaller part of a whole thing
AMELMIRO — **memorial** — a building or statue that honors someone who has died
BEARLM — **marble** — what Lincoln's statue is made of

Page 47

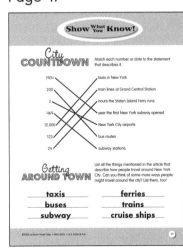

Show What You Know!

City Countdown

Match each number or date to the statement that describes it.

1904 — taxis in New York
200 — train lines at Grand Central Station
2 — hours the Staten Island Ferry runs
469 — year the first New York subway opened
12,000 — New York City airports
123 — bus routes
24 — subway stations

Getting Around Town

List all the things mentioned in the article that describe how people travel around New York City. Can you think of some more ways people might travel around the city? List them, too!

taxis — **ferries**
buses — **trains**
subway — **cruise ships**

Page 48

Page 49

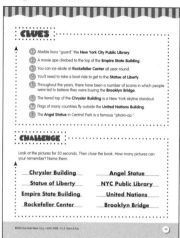

Page 51

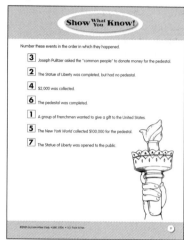

Page 52

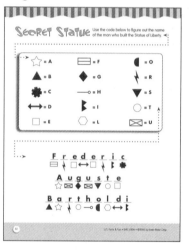

Page 53

Page 55

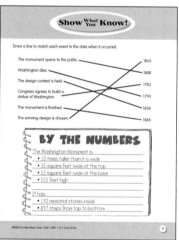

Page 56

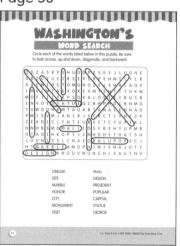

Page 57

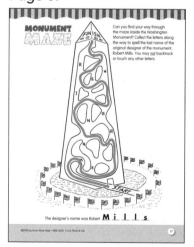

Page 59

Page 61

Norman Rockwell painted more pictures of Abraham Lincoln than any other president. You can draw your own picture of Lincoln. Copy each square from the grid on page 60 into the same place on this grid to create your picture. Then color the picture.

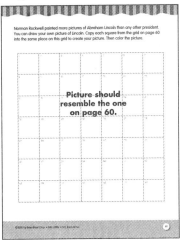

Picture should resemble the one on page 60.

Page 63

Show What You Know!

Write whether each statement is true or false.

1. **false** — Figure was a big strong horse.
2. **false** — Figure was born around 1700.
3. **true** — Figure's original owner gave him to a cousin to repay a debt.
4. **true** — Figure won many log-pulling contests.
5. **false** — Figure lost a lot of races.
6. **false** — The Morgan horse started in Europe.
7. **false** — During his life, Figure was not famous.
8. **true** — Figure lived to be about 30 years old.
9. **true** — The Morgan horse continues to be popular today.

Page 64

WORD SCRAMBLES

Reread paragraphs three and four of the story. Underline the words that describe Figure, the first Morgan horse. Then write the words below.

small	friendly
tough	handsome
racehorse	gentle
strong	famous
fast	

Use the words you wrote to unscramble the words below.

LFIEYRDN	FRIENDLY
ETEGNL	GENTLE
LSALM	SMALL
NRSOGT	STRONG
DAHOEMSN	HANDSOME
TAFS	FAST
UMASFO	FAMOUS

Page 65

A DIFFERENT HORSE

Can you find and circle the one horse that is not the same as the others? On the lines, write a sentence that tells what makes this horse different.

This horse has its right front leg wrapped.

Page 67

Show What You Know!

Number the following events in order from the event that happened first to the event that happened last.

7 — The Liberty Bell cracked when rung to announce the death of John Marshall.
2 — The bell arrived in Philadelphia from London.
8 — The Liberty Bell's chime was carried across the country in the first coast-to-coast telephone call.
4 — The bell was melted down and copper was added.
1 — A bell was ordered from England.
6 — The bell was rung to announce the signing of the Declaration of Independence.
3 — The bell cracked for the first time.
5 — Tin was added to make the bell sound better.

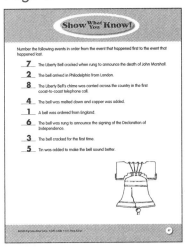

Page 68

Liberty Bell Word Games

Word Squares

Each bell contains an 8-letter word from the story. Find each word by starting at one of the letters and reading either clockwise or counterclockwise. Then write the words on the lines.

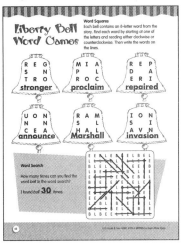

stronger   proclaim   repaired

announce   Marshall   invasion

Word Search

How many times can you find the word bell in the word search?

I found bell **30** times.

Page 69

Spell It Out

Read about the place where the Liberty Bell was displayed for many years. Cross out every third letter to uncover the name. Write the answer on the line.

I N E D E Y P E W N D P E N F C E E H A X L L O

Independence Hall

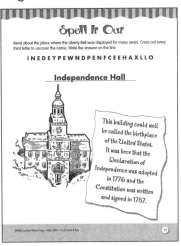

This building could well be called the birthplace of the United States. It was here that the Declaration of Independence was adopted in 1776 and the Constitution was written and signed in 1787.

Page 71

Show What You Know!

Answer the questions.

1. Who picked the site for the new U.S. capital?
   George Washington
2. Why was the site picked?
   located in the middle of the 13 colonies
3. Who designed the nation's capital?
   Pierre L'Enfant
4. What three things did the design include?
   wide streets
   long mall
   parks and open spaces
5. In what year did John Adams move into the White House?
   1800
6. Who is the capital named after?
   George Washington
7. What does the "D.C." in "Washington, D.C." stand for?
   District of Columbia
8. What three groups are honored with monuments in our nation's capital?
   American presidents
   soldiers
   important people

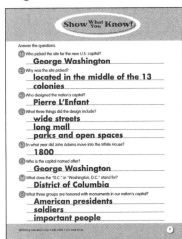

Page 72

A Visit to WASHINGTON, D.C.

Put on your walking shoes! Today, you're going to stroll through Washington, D.C. and visit some of the many famous landmarks—monuments, museums, and famous government buildings located there. Use the landmarks map on page 73 to complete the questions.

1. The Ellipse is an oval-shaped open area. It is located between which two famous landmarks? **The White House** **Washington Monument**
2. The highest court in the nation is located in Washington, D.C. What is its name?
   Supreme Court
   What major government building is it located behind? **Library of Congress**
3. Which memorial on the map honors war veterans?
   Vietnam Veterans Memorial
4. Name the long, narrow open area where many museums are located.
   The National Mall
5. If you visit the National Archives, you can see the original Declaration of Independence, the Constitution, and the Bill of Rights. What number is the National Archives on the map? **9**
   Is it north or south of the National Mall? **north**
6. The memorial to Thomas Jefferson, third president of the U.S., is located near three bodies of water. Name them.
   Tidal Basin **Washington Channel** **Potomac River**

Page 73

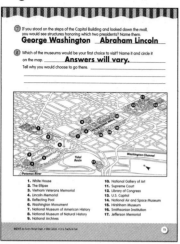

27. If you stood on the steps of the Capitol Building and looked down the mall, you would see structures honoring which two presidents? Name them.
George Washington   Abraham Lincoln

28. Which of the museums would be your first choice to visit? Name it and circle it on the map. **Answers will vary.**
Tell why you would choose to go there.

Map legend:
1. White House
2. The Ellipse
3. Vietnam Veterans Memorial
4. Lincoln Memorial
5. Reflecting Pool
6. Washington Monument
7. National Museum of American History
8. National Museum of Natural History
9. National Archives
10. National Gallery of Art
11. Supreme Court
12. Library of Congress
13. U.S. Capitol
14. National Air and Space Museum
15. Hirshhorn Museum
16. Smithsonian Institution
17. Jefferson Memorial

Page 75

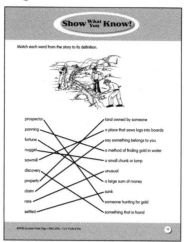

Show What You Know!

Match each word from the story to its definition.

prospector — someone hunting for gold
panning — a method of finding gold in water
fortune — a large sum of money
nugget — a small chunk or lump
sawmill — a place that saws logs into boards
discovery — something that is found
property — land owned by someone
claim — say something belongs to you
rare — unusual
settled — sank

Page 79

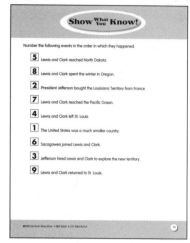

Show What You Know!

Number the following events in the order in which they happened.

5 Lewis and Clark reached North Dakota.
8 Lewis and Clark spent the winter in Oregon.
2 President Jefferson bought the Louisiana Territory from France.
7 Lewis and Clark reached the Pacific Ocean.
4 Lewis and Clark left St. Louis.
1 The United States was a much smaller country.
6 Sacagawea joined Lewis and Clark.
3 Jefferson hired Lewis and Clark to explore the new territory.
9 Lewis and Clark returned to St. Louis.

Page 80

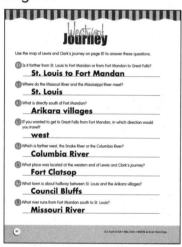

Westward Journey

Use the map of Lewis and Clark's journey on page 81 to answer these questions.

1. Is it farther from St. Louis to Fort Mandan or from Fort Mandan to Great Falls?
St. Louis to Fort Mandan

2. Where do the Missouri River and the Mississippi River meet?
St. Louis

3. What is directly south of Fort Mandan?
Arikara villages

4. If you wanted to get to Great Falls from Fort Mandan, in which direction would you travel?
west

5. Which is farther west, the Snake River or the Columbia River?
Columbia River

6. What place was located at the western end of Lewis and Clark's journey?
Fort Clatsop

7. What town is about halfway between St. Louis and the Arikara villages?
Council Bluffs

8. What river runs from Fort Mandan south to St. Louis?
Missouri River

Page 83

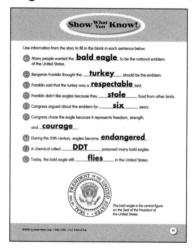

Show What You Know!

Use information from the story to fill in the blank in each sentence below.

1. Many people wanted the **bald eagle** to be the national emblem of the United States.
2. Benjamin Franklin thought the **turkey** should be the emblem.
3. Franklin said that the turkey was a **respectable** bird.
4. Franklin didn't like eagles because they **stole** food from other birds.
5. Congress argued about the emblem for **six** years.
6. Congress chose the eagle because it represents freedom, strength, and **courage**.
7. During the 20th century, eagles became **endangered**.
8. A chemical called **DDT** poisoned many bald eagles.
9. Today, the bald eagle still **flies** in the United States.

The bald eagle is the central figure on the Seal of the President of the United States.

Page 84

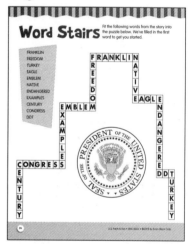

Word Stairs

Fit the following words from the story into the puzzle below. We've filled in the first word to get you started.

FRANKLIN
FREEDOM
TURKEY
EAGLE
EMBLEM
NATIVE
ENDANGERED
EXAMPLES
CENTURY
CONGRESS
DDT

Page 85

Gone Fishin'

An eagle's sharp eyesight lets it see fish swimming in rivers far below. Help this eagle find a salmon for dinner.

"Hey, Little Fishy, Come Out, Come Out wherever you are . . ."

Page 87

Show What You Know!

Write yes next to the animals that the story says live in the Everglades. Write no next to the animals that don't live there.

yes alligator   yes snake
no woodchuck   no kangaroo
yes bald eagle   no horse
yes bear   yes egret
no penguin   yes bobcat
yes anhinga   no camel
yes manatee   no tiger
yes panther   yes crocodile

Look at the animals that you wrote yes beside. Then write each animal's name in the group to which it belongs.

Reptiles	Birds	Mammals
alligator	bald eagle	bear
snake	anhinga	manatee
crocodile	egret	panther
		bobcat

Page 88

EVERGLADES SCRAMBLE

Unscramble the words below and write them on the lines. Then unscramble the shaded letters to find out a way to travel through the Everglades.

HINT: The number after each scrambled word tells you the paragraph where the word can be found.

ABTOCB (2) **BOBCAT**
AFIRLOD (1) **FLORIDA**
GANIWD (2) **WADING**
EADMAG (3) **DAMAGE**
AKPR (4) **PARK**
NENREEDAGD (4) **ENDANGERED**
ERWTA (1) **WATER**

Shaded letters: **B O I A R A T**
Way to travel: **A I R B O A T**
HINT: what you breathe   HINT: another word for ship

Page 89

Page 91

Page 92

Answers may vary.

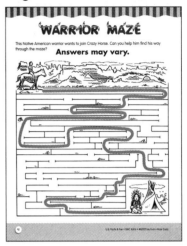

Page 93

Page 95

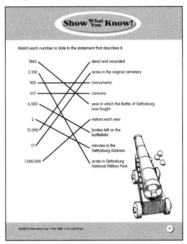

Page 96

Page 97

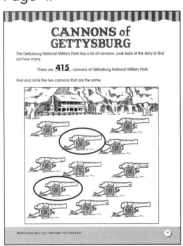

Page 99

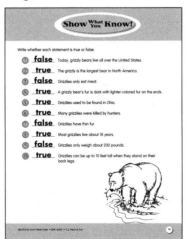

Page 100

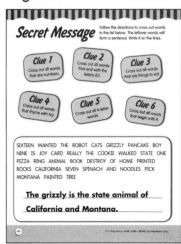

Page 101

Hidden Grizzlies

Can you find eight hidden grizzly bears hiding in this picture? Color them.

"Let's stop and rest here, boy. There don't seem to be any bears around."

Page 103

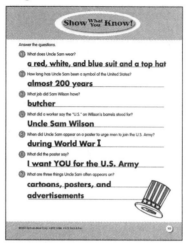

Show What You Know!

Answer the questions.

1. What does Uncle Sam wear?
a red, white, and blue suit and a top hat
2. How long has Uncle Sam been a symbol of the United States?
almost 200 years
3. What job did Sam Wilson have?
butcher
4. What did a worker say the "U.S." on Wilson's barrels stood for?
Uncle Sam Wilson
5. When did Uncle Sam appear on a poster to urge men to join the U.S. Army?
during World War I
6. What did the poster say?
I want YOU for the U.S. Army
7. What are three things Uncle Sam often appears on?
cartoons, posters, and advertisements

Page 104

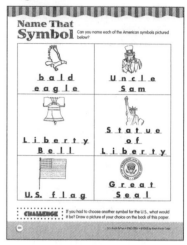

Name That Symbol Can you name each of the American symbols pictured below?

bald eagle

Uncle Sam

Liberty Bell

Statue of Liberty

U.S. flag

Great Seal

CHALLENGE If you had to choose another symbol for the U.S., what would it be? Draw a picture of your choice on the back of this paper.

Page 105

Math Clues

Solve each math problem below. Then use the answers to figure out the code and discover the name of the man who designed the World War I poster of Uncle Sam.

92 − 48 = **44**
70 × 4 = **280**
43 × 2 = **86**
65 + 15 = **80**
73 − 39 = **34**
34 + 59 = **93**
9 × 15 = **135**
85 × 3 = **255**
16 × 6 = **96**
48 − 43 = **55**
54 − 29 = **29**
84 + 13 = **102**
87 + 41 = **128**

J A M E S
80 29 93 135

M O N T G O M E R Y
93 102 96 255 55 102 93 34 128 280

F L A G G
44 86 29 55 55

Page 107

Show What You Know!

Number the following events in the order in which they happened.

4 Ellis Island fell into decay.
6 Restoration organizers came up with a special way to raise money.
7 The Ellis Island Immigration Museum opened.
2 Changing laws reduced the number of immigrants passing through Ellis Island.
5 Plans were made to restore the island.
1 Ellis Island Immigration Station opened.
8 Ellis Island is one of America's most popular historical sites.
3 Ellis Island closed.

Page 108

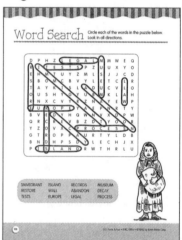

Word Search Circle each of the words in the puzzle below. Look in all directions.

IMMIGRANT · ISLAND · RECORDS · MUSEUM
RESTORE · WALL · ABANDON · DECAY
TESTS · EUROPE · LEGAL · PROCESS

Page 109

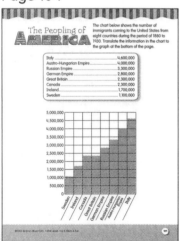

The Peopling of AMERICA

The chart below shows the number of immigrants coming to the United States from eight countries during the period of 1880 to 1930. Translate the information in the chart to the graph at the bottom of the page.

Italy 4,600,000
Austro-Hungarian Empire ... 4,000,000
Russian Empire 3,300,000
German Empire 2,800,000
Great Britain 2,300,000
Canada 2,300,000
Ireland 1,700,000
Sweden 1,100,000

Page 111

Show What You Know!

Fill in the blanks with the word from the story that completes the sentence.

1. Rosa Parks lived in Montgomery, **Alabama**.
2. The buses in Montgomery were **segregated**.
3. Rosa refused to give up her **seat** to a white man.
4. Rosa was **arrested** for refusing to get up.
5. Rosa's friends organized a bus **boycott**.
6. Blacks had to walk, share rides, or take **cabs**.
7. They faced anger and **violence** from some white people.
8. On November 13, 1956, the **Supreme** Court said segregation was against the law.
9. From that day on, blacks and whites had to be treated **equally** on city buses.
10. Rosa Parks is called the "**mother** of the civil rights movement."

Page 113

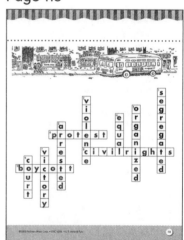

(crossword puzzle)

violent
protest
organized
civil rights
segregated
boycott
victory
court

Page 115

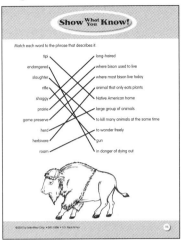

Show What You Know!

Match each word to the phrase that describes it.

- tipi — long-haired
- endangered — where bison used to live
- slaughter — where most bison live today
- rifle — animal that only eats plants
- shaggy — Native American home
- prairie — large group of animals
- game preserve — to kill many animals at the same time
- herd — to wander freely
- herbivore — gun
- roam — in danger of dying out

Page 116

Baffled Bison

Can you find the two bison that are exactly alike? Draw a circle around them.

Page 117

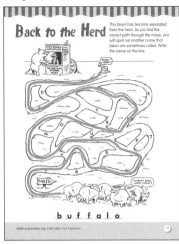

Back to the Herd

This bison has become separated from the herd. As you find the correct path through the maze, you will spell out another name that bison are sometimes called. Write the name on the line.

b u f f a l o

Page 119

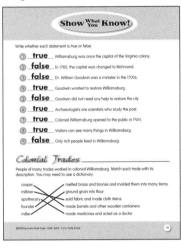

Show What You Know!

Write whether each statement is true or false.

1. **true** — Williamsburg was once the capital of the Virginia colony.
2. **false** — In 1785, the capital was changed to Richmond.
3. **false** — Dr. William Goodwin was a minister in the 1700s.
4. **true** — Goodwin wanted to restore Williamsburg.
5. **false** — Goodwin did not need any help to restore the city.
6. **true** — Archaeologists are scientists who study the past.
7. **true** — Colonial Williamsburg opened to the public in 1934.
8. **true** — Visitors can see many things in Williamsburg.
9. **false** — Only rich people lived in Williamsburg.

Colonial Trades

People of many trades worked in colonial Williamsburg. Match each trade with its description. You may need to use a dictionary.

- cooper — melted brass and bronze and molded them into many items
- milliner — ground grain into flour
- apothecary — sold fabric and made cloth items
- founder — made barrels and other wooden containers
- miller — made medicines and acted as a doctor

Page 120

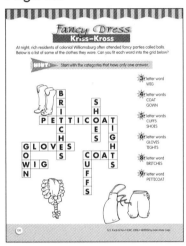

Fancy Dress Kriss-Kross

At night, rich residents of colonial Williamsburg often attended fancy parties called balls. Below is a list of some of the clothes they wore. Can you fit each word into the grid below?

HINT: Start with the categories that have only one answer.

- **3**-letter word: WIG
- **4**-letter words: COAT, GOWN
- **5**-letter words: CLIFFS, SHOES
- **6**-letter words: GLOVES, TIGHTS
- **8**-letter word: BRITCHES
- **9**-letter word: PETTICOAT

Page 121

Digging for History

Archaeologists found many old items when they dug into Williamsburg's past. Find the eight items hidden in the bottom of this old well. Color them.

hammer
plate
comb
shoe
spoon
mirror
doll
tea cup

Page 123

Show What You Know!

Write whether each statement is true or false.

1. **true** — The Wright brothers made the first flight at Kitty Hawk, North Carolina.
2. **true** — The Wright brothers liked to invent flying toys when they were young.
3. **false** — Gliders are planes with motors.
4. **false** — A plane's wings are curved.
5. **false** — The Wright brothers built only one glider.
6. **true** — The Wright brothers added a propeller and motor to a glider to create an airplane.
7. **false** — The brothers tested their plane in Dayton, Ohio.
8. **true** — Kitty Hawk was a windy, sandy place.
9. **false** — Wilbur flew the first airplane.
10. **false** — The first flight lasted several minutes.

Page 124

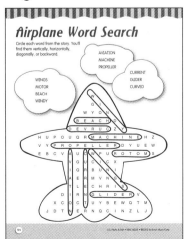

Airplane Word Search

Circle each word from the story. You'll find them vertically, horizontally, diagonally, or backward.

AVIATION
MACHINE
PROPELLER
WINGS
MOTOR
BEACH
WINDY
CURRENT
GLIDER
CURVED

Page 125

Airplane

How many words can you make out of the letters in AIRPLANE? Write as many as you can think of on the lines below.

Answers will vary.

air	ale	liar	pile
plane	rain	lain	ear
nail	pain	rail	pear
pail	lane	pearl	near
ail	panel	lip	pale

Make 8 words and you're an Orville Wright.

Make 13 words and you're a Chuck Yeager, the first pilot to fly faster than the speed of sound.

Make 20 or more words and you're a Neil Armstrong, the first person to step on the moon.

My score

I'm a **Answers will vary.**

Page 127

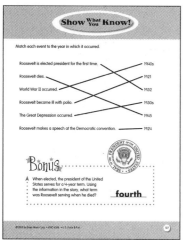

Show What You Know!

Match each event to the year in which it occurred.

Roosevelt is elected president for the first time. — 1940s
Roosevelt dies. — 1921
World War II occurred. — 1932
Roosevelt became ill with polio. — 1930s
The Great Depression occurred. — 1945
Roosevelt makes a speech at the Democratic convention. — 1924

Bonus

When elected, the president of the United States serves for a 4-year term. Using the information in the story, what term was Roosevelt serving when he died? **fourth**

Page 128

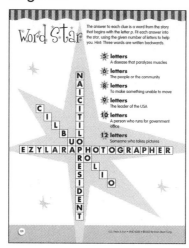

Word Star

The answer to each clue is a word from the story that begins with the letter p. Fit each answer into the star, using the given number of letters to help you. Hint: Three words are written backwards.

5 letters — A disease that paralyzes muscles
6 letters — The people or the community
8 letters — To make something unable to move
9 letters — The leader of the USA
10 letters — A person who runs for government office
12 letters — Someone who takes pictures

NAICITILOP / RESIDENT / CILBUP / OILOP / EZYLARAP / PHOTOGRAPHER

Page 129

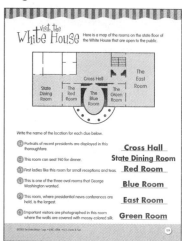

Visit the White House

Here is a map of the rooms on the state floor of the White House that are open to the public.

State Dining Room / The Red Room / The Blue Room / The Green Room / The East Room / Cross Hall

Write the name of the location for each clue below.

1. Portraits of recent presidents are displayed in this thoroughfare. — **Cross Hall**
2. This room can seat 140 for dinner. — **State Dining Room**
3. First ladies like this room for small receptions and teas. — **Red Room**
4. This is one of the three oval rooms that George Washington wanted. — **Blue Room**
5. This room, where presidential news conferences are held, is the largest. — **East Room**
6. Important visitors are photographed in this room where the walls are covered with mossy-colored silk. — **Green Room**

Page 131

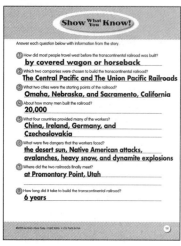

Show What You Know!

Answer each question below with information from the story.

1. How did most people travel west before the transcontinental railroad was built?
   by covered wagon or horseback
2. Which two companies were chosen to build the transcontinental railroad?
   The Central Pacific and The Union Pacific Railroads
3. What two cities were the starting points of the railroad?
   Omaha, Nebraska, and Sacramento, California
4. About how many men built the railroad?
   20,000
5. What four countries provided many of the workers?
   China, Ireland, Germany, and Czechoslovakia
6. What were five dangers that the workers faced?
   the desert sun, Native American attacks, avalanches, heavy snow, and dynamite explosions
7. Where did the two railroads finally meet?
   at Promontory Point, Utah
8. How long did it take to build the transcontinental railroad?
   6 years

Page 132

Hidden Words

Starting with the first letter, cross out every other letter to find out the following:

1. a way many people crossed the United States before the transcontinental railroad was built.
   XCHOYVWEARBECDPWYAEGXOMN
   COVERED WAGON
2. what the four businessmen who formed the Central Pacific Railroad were called, and
   YTPHRETBWIZGAFEOTUOR
   THE BIG FOUR
3. the name of one of these four businessmen who drove the golden spike at Promontory Point, and also founded a famous university in California.
   SLAEPLVARNOD MSOTCAWNYYFFOBRKD
   LELAND STANFORD

Page 133

Railroad Maze

Can you help the Central Pacific and the Union Pacific meet? Each railroad needs to get through the maze and meet at Promontory Point.

Page 135

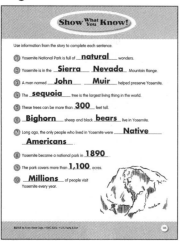

Show What You Know!

Use information from the story to complete each sentence.

1. Yosemite National Park is full of **natural** wonders.
2. Yosemite is in the **Sierra Nevada** Mountain Range.
3. A man named **John Muir** helped preserve Yosemite.
4. The **sequoia** tree is the largest living thing in the world.
5. These trees can be more than **300** feet tall.
6. **Bighorn** sheep and black **bears** live in Yosemite.
7. Long ago, the only people who lived in Yosemite were **Native Americans**.
8. Yosemite became a national park in **1890**.
9. The park covers more than **1,100** acres.
10. **Millions** of people visit Yosemite every year.

Page 136

Secret Message

Use the code below to discover an important message about visiting Yosemite National Park.

Z=A   S=H   I=R   V=E   K=P
Y=B   O=L   H=S   L=O
W=D   M=N   G=T   U=F

PLEASE DO NOT
KOVZHV   WL   MLG

FEED THE BEARS
UVVW   GSV   YVZIH

Bonus
On the back of this paper, create your own code. Write a message that gives a reason for the message above.

Page 137

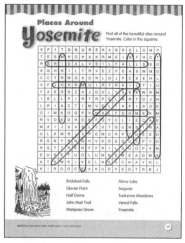

Places Around Yosemite

Find all of the beautiful sites around Yosemite. Color in the squares.

Bridalveil Falls
Glacier Point
Half Dome
John Muir Trail
Mariposa Grove
Mirror Lake
Sequoia
Tuolumne Meadows
Vernal Falls
Yosemite

Page 139

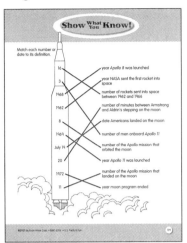

Show What You Know!

Match each number or date to its definition.

- 16 — number of minutes between Armstrong and Aldrin's stepping on the moon
- 3 — year NASA sent the first rocket into space
- 1968 — year Apollo 8 was launched
- 1962 — year NASA sent the first rocket into space
- 8 — number of rockets sent into space between 1962 and 1966
- 1969 — year Apollo 11 was launched
- July 19 — number of the Apollo mission that orbited the moon
- 20 — date Americans landed on the moon
- 1972 — number of men onboard Apollo 11
- 11 — year moon program ended

Page 143

Show What You Know!

Solve this kachina crossword puzzle.

Across
2. Kachinas are often decorated with **plants**
4. The Hopi believe that **spirits** are part of everyday life.
6. Kachinas are carved from the root of the **cottonwood** tree.
7. Kachinas are often shown holding **weapons**
8. Today, you can see kachina dolls in **museums**

Down
1. Kachinas are also called the "**cloud** people."
3. Artists decorate kachinas with items from **nature**
5. The Hopi use kachina dolls during religious **rituals**

Page 144

Colorful Kachinas

The Hopi painted their kachinas with colors made from natural materials. Earth tones as well as rainbow hues were used.

Color this kachina to make it appear as authentic as possible.

Should be colored with earth tones and bright colors.

Page 145

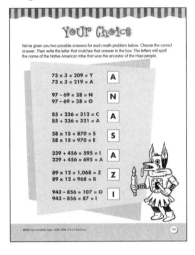

Your Choice

We've given you two possible answers for each math problem below. Choose the correct answer. Then write the letter that matches that answer in the box. The letters will spell the name of the Native American tribe that was the ancestor of the Hopi people.

- 73 × 3 = 209 = Y / 73 × 3 = 219 = A → **A**
- 97 − 69 = 28 = N / 97 − 69 = 38 = O → **N**
- 85 + 236 = 312 = C / 85 + 236 = 321 = A → **A**
- 58 × 15 = 870 = S / 58 × 15 = 970 = E → **S**
- 239 + 456 = 595 = I / 239 + 456 = 695 = A → **A**
- 89 × 12 = 1,068 = Z / 89 × 12 = 968 = R → **Z**
- 943 − 856 = 107 = O / 943 − 856 = 87 = I → **I**

Page 147

Show What You Know!

Write whether each statement is true or false.

1. **false** — The first European settlers in America arrived after 1700.
2. **false** — The settlers came to America for farmland.
3. **true** — The settlers named the James River and Jamestown after King James I of England.
4. **true** — The settlers came to America by ship.
5. **false** — The James River was a good source of fresh water.
6. **true** — Many settlers died during the first year.
7. **true** — Captain John Smith made friends with Native Americans who helped the settlers.
8. **true** — The Jamestown settlers grew tobacco and sold it to England.
9. **false** — Jamestown was full of gold and silver.
10. **true** — Jamestown was the first permanent English settlement in America.

Page 148

Jamestown Jumble

Unscramble each word below. The numbers will tell you the paragraph where the word appears in the story. Then unscramble the circled letters to find out the name of John Smith's Native American friend.

- RACEMIA (1) **AMERICA**
- VEATIN (4) **NATIVE**
- LGDO (1) **GOLD**
- KPSAEHEEAC (2) **CHESAPEAKE**
- CTAOCBO (4) **TOBACCO**
- STLSEERT (2) **SETTLERS**
- OONLITSCS (3) **COLONISTS**
- GHITIVNR (4) **THRIVING**
- PLUSPIES (4) **SUPPLIES**

Circled letters: **AAOPOTCNHS**

Answer: **POCAHONTAS**

Page 149

Jamestown Maze

This colonist has gotten lost in the woods! Can you help him find his way back to Jamestown?

Page 151

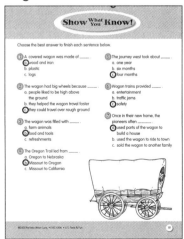

Show What You Know!

Choose the best answer to finish each sentence below.

1. A covered wagon was made of ____.
   a. wood and iron
   b. plastic
   c. logs
2. The wagon had big wheels because ____.
   a. people liked to be high above the ground
   b. they helped the wagon travel faster
   c. they could travel over rough ground
3. The wagon was filled with ____.
   a. farm animals
   b. food and tools
   c. refreshments
4. The Oregon Trail led from ____.
   a. Oregon to Nebraska
   b. Missouri to Oregon
   c. Missouri to California
5. The journey west took about ____.
   a. one year
   b. six months
   c. four months
6. Wagon trains provided ____.
   a. entertainment
   b. traffic jams
   c. safety
7. Once in their new home, the pioneers often ____.
   a. used parts of the wagon to build a house
   b. used the wagon to ride to town
   c. sold the wagon to another family

Page 152

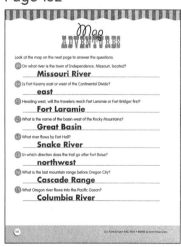

Map Adventure

Look at the map on the next page to answer the questions.

1. On what river is the town of Independence, Missouri, located? **Missouri River**
2. Is Fort Kearny east or west of the Continental Divide? **east**
3. Heading west, will the travelers reach Fort Laramie or Fort Bridger first? **Fort Laramie**
4. What is the name of the basin west of the Rocky Mountains? **Great Basin**
5. What river flows by Fort Hall? **Snake River**
6. In which direction does the trail go after Fort Boise? **northwest**
7. What is the last mountain range before Oregon City? **Cascade Range**
8. What Oregon river flows into the Pacific Ocean? **Columbia River**

Page 155

Show What You Know!

Draw a line to match each word on the right with the correct definition on the left.

a certain road or way — route
to flood over the edges — overflow
land along the sides of a river — banks
fast, rough water — rapids
rivers that flow into a larger river — tributaries
to damage badly — devastate
flat plain where a river deposits mud — delta
something valuable or useful — resource

ROLLIN' ON THE RIVER Mississippi riverboats were powered by steam that turned a large paddle wheel at the back of the boat. Unscramble the letters to find out a nickname for this type of boat.

NEWHTSEERELR

s t e r n w h e e l e r

Page 156

SCRAMBLED STATES The Mississippi flows by or through 10 states. Can you unscramble the name of each of these states below? Use the map on the next page to help you.

OMNTINEAS **M I N N E S O T A**

WIAO **I O W A**

SLOILINI **I L L I N O I S**

UNALSIOIA **L O U I S I A N A**

NISCWNOSI **W I S C O N S I N**

TNEUKCYK **K E N T U C K Y**

ASKSRANA **A R K A N S A S**

ENTNSEESE **T E N N E S S E E**

IPSMSISIPSI **M I S S I S S I P P I**

ORSISIMU **M I S S O U R I**

Page 157

A TRIP DOWN THE MISSISSIPPI Come journey down the 2,340-mile length of the Mississippi from its small beginnings. You'll see many interesting sites. Number these sights in the order you would see them.

3 Gateway Arch towering above the riverbanks at St. Louis

6 A Mardi Gras parade in this city near the Mississippi Delta

1 A small stream leaving Lake Itasca

7 Fishing boats heading out into the waters of the Gulf of Mexico

5 A Civil War memorial commemorating the Battle of Vicksburg

2 The Twin Cities, one on each side of the river

4 The largest city in Tennessee

Page 159

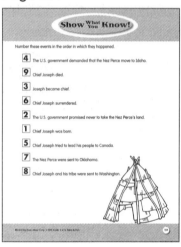

Show What You Know!

Number these events in the order in which they happened.

4 The U.S. government demanded that the Nez Perce move to Idaho.

9 Chief Joseph died.

3 Joseph became chief.

6 Chief Joseph surrendered.

2 The U.S. government promised never to take the Nez Perce's land.

1 Chief Joseph was born.

5 Chief Joseph tried to lead his people to Canada.

7 The Nez Perce were sent to Oklahoma.

8 Chief Joseph and his tribe were sent to Washington.

Page 160

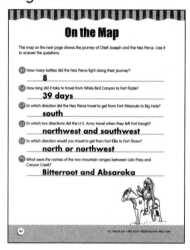

On the Map

The map on the next page shows the journey of Chief Joseph and the Nez Perce. Use it to answer the questions.

1. How many battles did the Nez Perce fight along their journey?
8

2. How long did it take to travel from White Bird Canyon to Fort Fizzle?
39 days

3. In which direction did the Nez Perce travel to get from Fort Missoula to Big Hole?
south

4. In which two directions did the U.S. Army travel when they left Fort Keogh?
northwest and southwest

5. In which direction would you travel to get from Fort Ellis to Fort Shaw?
north or northwest

6. What were the names of the two mountain ranges between Lolo Pass and Canyon Creek?
Bitterroot and Absaroka

Page 163

Show What You Know!

Write whether each statement is true or false.

1. **false** The first baseball game was played about 75 years ago.

2. **true** The first baseball game was played in New Jersey.

3. **false** The rules of baseball have always stayed the same.

4. **true** Babe Ruth was a popular home-run hitter for the New York Yankees.

5. **false** Many black Americans played in the Major Leagues before 1947.

6. **true** Jackie Robinson was the first black American to play in the Major Leagues.

7. **false** Only grown-ups can enjoy baseball.

8. **true** The Little League has its own World Series.

9. **true** Many children play baseball in their own neighborhoods.

10. **true** A scorecard is used to keep track of the action in a game.

Page 165

(Crossword puzzle with baseball team names: RedSox, Pirates, Diamondbacks, Cardinals, DevilRays, Rangers, Twins, Phillies, Angels, Orioles, Braves, Yankees, Marlins, Mets, Padres, etc.)

Page 167

Show What You Know!

Write the names of the Great Lakes from largest to smallest below.

1. Lake **S u p e r i o r**
2. Lake **H u r o n**
3. Lake **M i c h i g a n**
4. Lake **E r i e**
5. Lake **O n t a r i o**

Next, rearrange the boxed letters to spell the name of an area of wet, low-lying land around a lake.

Boxed letters **S H M R A**

Answer **M A R S H**

Now, rearrange the shaded letters to spell the name of the type of moss that grows in the area you spelled out above.

Shaded letters **p a e t**

Answer **p e a t**

Page 168

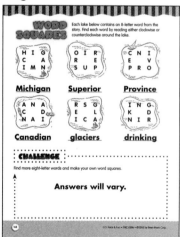

WORD SQUARES Each lake below contains an 8-letter word from the story. Find each word by reading either clockwise or counterclockwise around the lake.

Michigan   **Superior**   **Province**

Canadian   **glaciers**   **drinking**

CHALLENGE Find more eight-letter words and make your own word squares.

Answers will vary.

Page 169

Page 171

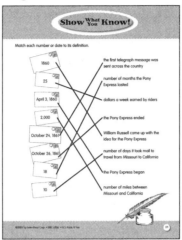

Page 172

Page 173

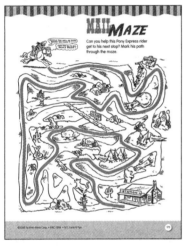

Page 175

Page 176

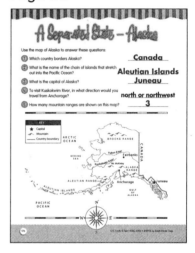

Page 177

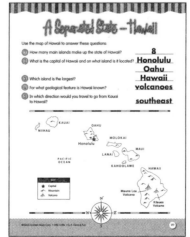